T0323951

A Modern Credit Rating Agency

This book aims to present a picture of one of the world's leading credit rating agencies. Credited as being the first credit rating agency, Moody's stands as the epitome of the rating sector and all that it effects. However, outside of internal and non-public histories compiled within the rating agency itself, the story of Moody's has never been told, until now. However, this is not a historical book. Rather, this book paints a picture of Moody's on a wider canvas that introduces the concept of rating to you, taking into account the origins of the sector, the competitive battles that formed the modern-day oligopoly, and the characters that have each taken their turn on sculpting the industry that, today, is critical to the modern economy.

The book is a story of personable people who provided the market with what it needed, but it is more than that. It is a story of conflict, impact, strategy, and most of all the relationship between big business and modern society. Standing as the gatekeeper to the capital markets that form the core of modern society, Moody's represents the very best of what the marketplace can produce, but also the very worst. This story takes in economic crises in the antebellum US, the Panics of the early 1900s, the Wall Street Crash and the Great Depression and, of course, the Global Financial Crisis. It does this because, at the heart of each one was a member of the rating industry or the reporting industry that preceded it. Associated with almost any financial scandal you may care to remember the credit rating agencies, in their often-uncomfortable role as gatekeepers, have their fingerprints on most financial scandals and calamities. This book tells the story of the industry's founding member.

Daniel Cash is Associate Professor at Aston University in the UK. He was a Fulbright Scholar from 2022 to 2023 at New York University's Stern Business School. He has authored eight books and almost thirty articles all on the credit rating industry and ESG rating industry, after receiving his PhD in 2016, within which he focused on the provision of ancillary services by credit rating agencies.

Routledge Studies in Corporate Governance

Corporate Governance in India
Arindam Das

Corporate Governance and Whistleblowing
Corporate Culture and Employee Behaviour
Moeen Umar Cheema, Rahat Munir and Sophia Su

Corporate Governance, Ownership Structure and Firm Performance
Mediation Models and Dynamic Approaches
Hoang N. Phan and Sardar M. N. Islam

Corporate Social Responsibility and Governance
Stakeholders, Management and Organizational Performance in the European
Union
Panagiotis Dimitropoulos and Efthalia Chatzigianni

Supply Chain Management and Corporate Governance
Artificial intelligence, game theory and robust optimization
Catherine Xiaocui Lou, Sardar M. N. Islam and Nicholas Billington

Corporate Governance and IFRS in the Middle East
Compliance with International Financial Reporting Standards
Muath Abdelqader, Tamer K. Darwish, and Khalil Nimer

A Modern Credit Rating Agency
The Story of Moody's
Daniel Cash

For more information about this series, please visit www.routledge.com/Routledge-Studies-in-Corporate-Governance/book-series/RSCG

A Modern Credit Rating Agency

The Story of Moody's

Daniel Cash

Routledge
Taylor & Francis Group

NEW YORK AND LONDON

First published 2024
by Routledge
605 Third Avenue, New York, NY 10158

and by Routledge
4 Park Square, Milton Park, Abingdon, Oxon, OX14 4RN

Routledge is an imprint of the Taylor & Francis Group, an informa business

© 2024 Taylor & Francis

ISBN: 978-0-367-42744-3 (hbk)
ISBN: 978-1-032-57572-8 (pbk)
ISBN: 978-1-003-00106-5 (ebk)

DOI: 10.4324/9781003001065

Typeset in Times New Roman
by Apex CoVantage, LLC

Contents

Preface

I am not sure whether it is prudent to start by detailing what a book *is not*, rather than what it *is*, but, anyway. I thought it may be of interest to explain the logic behind this book before you start to read; hopefully, it does not cause you to stop reading! My initial objective ever since I first became infected with the appetite to know all that I could about the sector that was identified as being at the heart of the systemic collapse that so affected everything in my environment – I was twenty years old when the Financial Crisis unfolded – was to write a history of Moody's. The fact that one of the main perpetrators was a public company, with everything laid bare for all to see (well, most things!) was so fascinating to me as I started my journey. I utilised the company's 'publicness' for my Doctoral Thesis where I tried to show that the rating agency's development of ancillary services (and, by proxy, the rest of the oligopoly members' too, although it is infinitely more difficult to ascertain the same level of information from them) provided an unnecessary and ill-earned cushion against whatever financial penalty would be coming their way; I was proven correct when the 'record' penalties of $1.3bn and $864mn to S&P and Moody's were dished out just before, and just after I completed the PhD, and were instantly absorbed by the agencies before swiftly moving on. Anyway, I digress. Digging into Moody's publicness and presenting the first-ever public history of the company was all that I wanted to do!

However, upon writing the book and delving into the often-murky world of speaking to former employees and analysts of the company, it quickly dawned on me that what I imagined for all of those years was not something I actually wanted to do. (I think we can all relate to that in one form or another!) An 'official' history existed already, albeit only available internally at Moody's and, without explaining too much, kept safe by former employees who will not, and likely cannot ever let it go public. That means one cannot cite it which, to me personally as I see research and what I want to do with my research, makes it entirely useless. But, at this point, I realised it was not the detailed history that was fascinating, but the *story*. The story of Moody's, as I have known it as I developed my own understanding through the years of exclusively researching the credit rating sector, is truly fascinating. To my mind the story, though I doubt

I could get a Hollywood executive to agree, is worthy of a movie! Therefore, if not a movie, then this book will have to suffice.

To that end, I set out on doing three things. First, I wanted to provide you, the reader, with something you could access that would give you the *feel* of Moody's. If you wanted just one resource to get a holistic feel of one of the main members of the credit rating sector, then I aimed to provide that resource. Second, I wanted to correct some of the accepted narratives that have unfortunately taken hold of the credit rating literature. There are some glaring oversights that have gone onto affect policy, unfortunately, and I thought this the perfect vehicle to at least address some of those aspects. Third, I wanted to present the story of Moody's as very much a story. I would hope I have achieved that and have managed to blend the factual with the taletelling and building of characters and connections, because Moody's story is very much dominated by strong, fascinating, and even sometimes entertaining characters but who are all intrinsically connected. A story that has characters who are, or at least who have claimed to be connected to Henry VIII, Benjamin Franklin, hired future Presidents into their business and who have played important roles in the abolition of slavery just to name a few elements but who are all connected by one business is surely worth a read! Yet, in truth, this is a story of a company, its origins, its progression, and its future that affects each and every one of us. Whether you reside near the Sahara, the Gobi, the Arabian or the Mojave deserts, or anywhere in between, the credit rating agencies affect you. It may be once, twice, or even more times removed from your everyday life but in some way, the credit rating agencies have a particular effect on your life and your fortunes. This is because they have become intrinsic and interwoven into the modern human system that revolves around the movement of capital. Getting to know who they are gives you the chance to know why certain aspects of your life are the way they are.

So, with all this in mind and more, I present to you *The Story of Moody's*.

Acknowledgements

I must start my acknowledgements by thanking my editorial team at Routledge. This book was years in the making but with the COVID-19 pandemic, my plans on utilising my conversations with those who had a deep knowledge on Moody's in particular, and credit ratings in general, were put on hold. With the US being the home of the international credit rating agencies, and New York being their actual home, I wanted to spend as much time in the City as I could to get a feel for the agency, its competition, and the sector moreover. I had dreamed of being able to write this book in particular ever since my PhD, and spending time in and around New York City always felt necessary. However, as international travel was not possible, my editorial team kindly supported my many requests to delay and delay again, something which I never do. Their support with the project from the very start has been incredibly helpful, important, and very simply massively appreciated.

I must also thank the Fulbright Commission and New York University's Stern Business School. The Fulbright Commission, in granting me the prestigious honour of being a full-award Fulbright Scholar for 2022–23, has given me a life-changing opportunity, the likes of which the younger version of myself could never have even imagined was possible for him. I owe more to the Fulbright Commission than I can ever possibly give back and their supporting of me and my vision for projects such as this has been genuinely remarkable. I would also like to thank Professor Lawrence (Larry) White, for supporting my development and being my sponsor at Stern Business School. He, along with his department's support staff (Amanda in particular) have been tireless in their supporting of my relentless questions, queries, and need for support as I made the move to New York. Based on many instances, my time at Stern Business School would not have been possible were it not for their support.

I must also thank the many, and I do mean many people who I have spoken to about this project. It was never my intention to formally interview any of them, nor ever even name them in terms of who I was speaking to. Very early on in my PhD I learned that the credit rating world has particular characteristics that define it, and not being on the record is one of them(!) I respected this. Yet, the people who helped me more than they likely know, and who I hope are reading this now, will know who they are. Their guiding me to find information, learn about what happened, and point me to my next victim(!) was fundamentally important to me being able to finish this project. My many years studying the credit rating industry exclusively have allowed me to tap into the undercurrent of the industry and its development, and those many conversations were vital aspects to that tutelage, for which I am eternally grateful.

I finish with an acknowledgement of my long-suffering other half, who suffers greatly when it is time to write. The toll on myself is considerable, but often it is greater for her. I am forever in her debt for her support.

1   Introduction

It is not difficult to find comments on the leading credit rating agencies in relation to their role in the Financial Crisis. Professor Lawrence White once wrote that:

> when the histories are written of the US subprime residential mortgage debacle of 2007–2008, and the world financial crisis that followed, the three large US-based credit-rating agencies – Moody's. Standard & Poor's, and Fitch – will surely be seen as central parties to the debacle, and rightly so.[1]

If we focus on Moody's in particular, then there were famous comments made which have stood the test of time, like this observation from Thomas Freidman:

> In fact, you could almost say that we live again in a two-superpower world. There is the U.S. and there is Moody's. The U.S. can destroy a country by levelling it with bombs; Moody's can destroy a country by downgrading its bonds.[2]

However, what does this mean to you if you are unfamiliar with the credit rating agencies? If you are not familiar, it may seem like a particularly evocative statement that is probably not accurately attributed to a financial industry recording revenues of billions of dollars. If you are familiar, then the actions and involvement of the credit rating agencies will be known, but the question then becomes 'how important were they?'. Either way, this book has the aim of presenting one of the leading credit rating agencies to you in all its glory. Starting from the time of its inception and moving forward to today, this book represents the first detailed examination of Moody's anywhere in the literature. We will focus on Moody's as it is the only rating agency that is currently, or that has ever been a wholly public company, meaning that we can access all of its financial records and organisational structure. But, why would we want to?

Perhaps, the answer to that question relates to the concept of perspective. One may believe that the agencies were, as White states, central to the Financial Crisis and, thus, should be examined in excruciating detail so that the potential for

DOI: 10.4324/9781003001065-1

re-offending is limited through increased awareness. Others may be interested in the development of the agency from a business perspective, from developing an industry-defining practice in the early 1900s, to facing extinction in the 1960s, to now recording revenues of billions of dollars. Regulators may be interested in analysing patterns so that they can better design future regulations tasked with providing safety to the marketplace. Whatever the perspective, the story of Moody's is a fascinating one and throughout the course of this book we will be introduced to a truly unique industry via one of its defining players. Therefore, this work has two clear Research Questions, if you will. The first is 'who are Moody's?' It is easy to discuss 'credit rating agencies' and include Moody's as one component of the so-called 'Big Three', but who are they? What is their history, and how, if at all, does that factor into their *character*? Second, can this analysis tell us anything about whether their pre-Crisis behaviour may be described accurately as 'legacy' issues?[3] The concept of 'legacy issues' points towards a behaviour that existed in the past and, therefore, no longer needs to be considered in relation to an entity's current and future performance. Whilst it may be comfortable for Moody's and other financial institutions to self-prescribe past behaviour as 'legacy issues', people analysing these institutions cannot be afforded such a luxury. It is very important that we consider whether those behaviours were indeed part of the era of hubris, or whether they may be engrained within the fibres of the company or industry itself – if the reality is the latter, then understanding the companies/industries in excruciating detail can help to provide guidance for future analyses and even regulatory strategies.

In lowering the curtain between author and reader for one moment, it has been a difficult decision regarding the structure that this book will take. There is a need to focus on the crisis era as it defined and continues to define how the credit rating industry is viewed, used, and treated. However, focusing on that era provides just a snapshot of the industry, and of Moody's, which almost fundamentally constrains the potential impact of this work. But, if we were to just assess Moody's genealogically, from its inception to today, there would be a need to deviate from the linear analysis too much. It is for that reason that we will be making three particular 'stops' on our journey so that the analysis is as linear as possible whilst remaining of interest. The first aspect required is some context for the book, so within this introduction, we will quickly assess the crisis era and conclude the introduction with the perceived failings of the credit rating agencies. Doing this will allow us to understand the importance of credit rating agencies by examining their impact. The connection between the rating agencies and the financial crisis is well-researched and widely acknowledged, but of course, it was not the only 'cause'; in analysing a number of other 'causes' we will be able to see that there were many interconnecting parts to the Financial Crisis and that the rating agencies were themselves a constituent part. There have been many pieces written about the credit rating agencies before, during, and definitely after the Financial Crisis, and all either quickly skirt over what a credit rating agency does or provide a 'primer' which seeks to anchor the analysis that invariably follows. We will take a different approach here and in essence provide a storied historical account of one of the Big Three for the first time.

That history will be divided into three clear sections for this book: from inception to the 1970s; the lead-up to the Financial Crisis Era; and then the Financial Crisis era and the aftermath. Having these waypoints will be important for us as we develop an analysis that seeks to provide a catalogue of examinations that can be viewed together to form, potentially, a pattern. If that pattern can be developed, then the effect may be important for a generalised understanding of the industry, but also for a regulatory view of the industry. Yet, this approach of a historical story pinned by three waypoints is not as straightforward as it seems.

Historical scholars, who concentrate on Business History more specifically, have suggested there are certain aims when undertaking research through this methodological prism. Decker, Kipping, and Wadhwani state that 'historical research, for instance, is often aimed at uncovering sequences and processes, rather than verifying specific claims',[4] which serves us well when we consider our aim is to present a holistic picture from within which you may be able to ascertain patterns that accentuate your understanding of the agency moving forward. The scholars support the approach taken in this book by declaring that:

> historians typically do not – or at least should not – treat information from the past as objectively accessible data that can be agglomerated into larger analytical models, but as sources that need to be critically understood and interpreted within the context of their creation and storage . . . historians usually interpret their subjects by creating periodisations and by moving back and forth in chronological time.[5]

This is an important sentiment, because within this book there will be many occasions where we need to delve backwards to move forward. It is also vitally important that the environments within which decisions were taken are acknowledged and contextualised appropriately, because the scholars' correct understanding is directly relatable to the changing context that surrounds Moody's history, as we shall see. Whilst this author is not a historian, a multi-disciplinary approach is not only wise but necessary when attempting to achieve what this book is attempting to achieve.

In that same multi-disciplinary vein, there is a need to consider *how* this aim will be met. There is a potential to utilise certain theories and have them sit as the major methodological lenses through which we would analyse Moody's, and they may well be useful. The McKinsey 7S model, as it is so-called, suggests that a 'firm is the comprehensive sum of its parts' and breaks a company down into seven distinct sections that we could then use as the framework to assess Moody's as a corporation (Strategy, Structure, Systems, Staff, Style, Skills, and Shared Values).[6] Alternatively, or perhaps additionally, we could use the 'Strategic Triangle' method which develops three key areas which managers should focus on and, in turn, would provide us with a clear methodology to again assess Moody's with (whether the purpose of the company is publicly valuable, whether it will be politically and legally supported, and whether it is administratively and operationally feasible).[7] This would of course need to be amended for our purposes and would only really be relatable to the decision faced by Warren Buffett in 2000. Yet, these theories from the world of operational research would be useful but would not allow us to fully achieve our goal. For that, we must step back from the complexity (on the face of it at least) and understand the importance of *telling a story*.

It may feel counterintuitive for an academic researcher to admit to wanting to 'tell a story', but in this instance, it may actually be advantageous. Rooney, Lawlor, and Rohan suggest that 'practically, they [stories] provide a framework through which we can investigate experience and gain access to the complexity of human affairs and human activity'.[8] Sounds like a direct fit. However, in understanding the fact that the research into the telling of a narrative and a story, which are different, stems from the fields of literary criticism, rhetorical theory, and poetics, the scholars state that 'in simple terms, a story is what someone tells and a narrative is a researcher's account of what someone tells'.[9] In that case, the approach that will be helpful for achieving our goal is to tell a *narrative* of Moody's by combining the literature of what is understood of its history with the information available through its public records. There is an advantage to this approach. As Liu, Xing, and Starik suggest, after Abbott coined the term 'narrative positivism', 'narrative analysis assesses the causal relationship between organisational events and attributes of relationships among agents and social actors. This in turn significantly influenced process theories and organisational change scholars'.[10] The scholars continue by declaring that 'scholars who write about organisations tell stories'. That conflicts with the delineation between telling a story and telling a narrative as established above, but the sentiment is the same. So, if the method is to tell a narrative, where should that start? Rather than start at the very beginning, it is worth jumping forward to the Financial Crisis to briefly acquaint ourselves with the reason for this book.

1.1 The Financial Crisis and the Entrance of the Agencies Onto the World Stage

The title of this subsection suggests that the Financial Crisis was the event that brought the credit rating agencies to the world stage. If you know of the credit rating agencies before reading this book, then you will know that this is not an accurate understanding. However, whilst the credit rating agencies had a substantial presence within the knowledge of those concerned with the marketplace before the Crisis, the events of 2007/2008 brought the credit rating agencies into the *public consciousness* for the first time. There have been a number of movies and documentaries that have brought the realities of the financial market-place into the living rooms of society, including *Too Big to Fail*, *Inside Job*, *Wall Street: Money Never Sleeps*, *Margin Call*, and perhaps the most well-received movie *The Big Short*.[11] This represented a massive demarcation in the history of the credit rating agencies who had been, for the majority of their history, perceptively rather small players within the wider financial game. However, the Financial Crisis would prove to be a turning point in the history of rating agencies. Understanding why means that we must first understand the purpose of a rating agency.

We will learn more about the purpose of a rating agency in the next chapter and as we continue to learn about the Financial Crisis, but as a rough starting point it is enough to know that a credit rating agency exists to give an opinion on the likelihood that a given debt will be repaid, on time and in full. Put in those terms, it all sounds remarkably simple. When the first commercialised credit (reporting) agency was created in the 1830s, that simplistic purpose was its sole mandate. However, modern-day agencies exist in a world of 'conscious complexity'[12] that has, in turn, served to complicate the service which they offer to the financial marketplace. The Financial Crisis, which embodies this concept of conscious complexity, provides us with an ideal lens with which to understand why the credit rating agencies have been catapulted into the public consciousness, and it is a fascinating story.

However, the story of the Financial Crisis is not a straightforward one to tell. It should come as no surprise that a crisis that enveloped much of the globe had a number of factors which caused it to exist. It would be short-sighted to suggest that there were a capped number of factors that caused the Crisis, and the literature on the era suggests that there are a multitude of reasons behind it. These range from simple economic analyses, to examinations of corporate greed and white-collar crime,[13] and everything else in between. With the constraints of this book in mind, it is necessary to be selective rather than analyse every suggested cause within the literature. This should not be understood to be a reflection on the usefulness of the analyses not selected, as subjects such as Behavioural Psychology,[14] Criminology,[15] Sociology,[16] and even Linguistics[17] are all incredibly useful in building a holistic picture of one of the most impactful eras upon modern humanity. Yet, the major US Congressional Investigations after the Crisis perhaps allow us to chart a pathway for telling the story of the Financial Crisis, as the main Congressional investigation notes a certain number of factors that contributed to the Crisis, and we shall assess them in turn. They were:

- The rise of 'Too-Big-To-Fail' Financial Institutions;
- An Increase in Mortgage Lending, and a shared increase in the role of 'Government-Sponsored Enterprises';
- And the development of the Structured Finance Market, and the role of the Credit Rating Agencies.

These are the main factors that the investigation deemed was the 'background' to the Crisis, although there are a large number of other issues examined in the 600+ page report.[18] There was also a clear focus within the investigation on a lack of Governmental oversight, but for our purposes, we shall address that issue within the different subsections because, as one would imagine when assessing such a massive economic collapse, the lack of oversight was pervasive. Before we analyse these factors in more detail, it is worth providing ourselves with a map of the Crisis so that the analysis is well pegged to the overarching story. With the help of the Congressional investigation, and also via a number of business press outlets, Figure 1.1 represents a timeline of the events surrounding the Financial Crisis as it existed across the North-Atlantic.[19] This timeline, when viewed in conjunction with the following subsections, allows us to both chart the development of the Crisis and also see when a number of factors that caused the Crisis began to affect the course of events.

1.2 The Rise of 'Too-Big-to-Fail' Financial Institutions

During the height of the Financial Crisis, the headlines were focused on the ever-disintegrating faith in the marketplace.[20] However, as the Governments on both sides of the Atlantic Ocean began pumping money into their respective financial systems, the issue of 'too-big-to-fail' and its dangers,[21] but also its appropriateness,[22] began filling the column inches. For the Senate and its post-Crisis investigation, it was clear that with the concept of 'too-big-to-fail' in the banking sector having become a reality in the US after a series of regulatory moves over a relatively short amount of time, 'some U.S. financial institutions [had] not only grown larger and more complex, but [had] also engaged in higher risk activities'.[23] This assessment points towards the issue of why such institutions would engage in riskier behaviour and the probable answer lies in the concept of 'too-big-to-fail' (TBTF).

Too-big-to-fail, as a concept, is not solely concerned with the banking sector. There are, as one might expect, a number of differing terminologies that describe the different stages of the same process – terms such as 'government bailouts' and 'lender of last resort' describe different elements of the same concept. However, the effect is still the same. For example, Leathers and Raines note how the wider term of 'government bailout' has been used in a variety of circumstances, like when in 1971 the US Government provided Lockheed Martin with $250 million in loan guarantees to prevent its failure. In 1979, the US Government provided $1.5 billion in loan guarantees to Chrysler, whilst in 1976 the bankrupt Penn Central Railroad was consolidated by the US Government for almost $7 billion. The authors note also how airlines, in the wake of the 9/11 Terrorist Attacks, received billions in Governmental funds.[24] In the wake of the Financial Crisis, when the focus was on the financial industries, the American automotive industry received billions of dollars in aid from the US Government.[25] Leathers and Raines rightly note that this concept is not just a modern one, with the British

December 2006
Ownit Mortgage Solutions goes
  bankrupt

February 27, 2007
Freddie Mac announces it will no longer
  buy the most risky subprime mortgages

March 7, 2007
FDIC issues cease and desist order against
  Fremont for unsafe and unsound banking

April 2, 2007
New Century bankruptcy

June 17, 2007
Two Bear Sterns Subprime Hedge funds
  collapse

July 10 and 12, 2007
Credit rating agencies issue first mass ratings
  downgrades of hundreds of RMBS and
  CDO Securities

August 6, 2007
American Home Mortgage bankruptcy

August 9, 2007
BNP Paribas halts redemptions on three
  funds – cannot measure the value of CDOs

August 31, 2007
Ameriquest Mortgage ceases operations

September 14, 2007
Fifth-largest British Mortgage lender suffers
  run – falls into state ownership in
  February 2008

January 11, 2008
Countrywide announces sale to Bank of
  America

January 30, 2008
S&P Downgrades or places on 'credit watch'
  over 8,000 RMBS and CDOs

March 24, 2008
Federal Reserve Bank of New York forms
  Maiden Lane 1 to help JPMorgan Chase
  acquire Bear Sterns

May 29, 2008
Bear Sterns shareholders approve sale

July 11, 2008
IndyMac Bank fails and is seized by FDIC

July 15, 2008
SEC restricts naked Short-Selling of some
  financial stocks

September 7, 2008
The US takes control of Fannie Mae
  and Freddie Mac

September 15, 2008
Lehman Brothers files for
  bankruptcy

September 15, 2008
Merrill Lynch announces its sale to
  Bank of America

September 16, 2008
Federal Reserve offers $85 billion
  credit line to AIG

September 17, 2008
The UK's largest Mortgage
  Lender, HBoS, is rescued by
  Lloyds TSB

September 21, 2008
Goldman Sachs and Morgan
  Stanley convert to bank holding
  companies

September 25, 2008
Washington Mutual (WaMu) is
  seized by the FDIC and is sold to
  JPMorgan Chase

October 3, 2008
The US establishes the Troubled
  Asset Relief Program (TARP)

October 7–8, 2008
Iceland's three largest commercial
  banks collapse – the UK uses anti-
  Terror Legislation to freeze their
  assets in the UK

October 12, 2008
Wachovia is sold to Wells Fargo

October 13, 2008
The UK bails out RBS and Lloyds
  TSB amongst others

October 28, 2008
The US uses TARP and buys
  $125 billion in preferred stock
  from 9 banks

November 25, 2008
Federal Reserve buys Fannie Mae
  and Freddie Mac's Assets

May 2, 2010
Greece is bailed out by the EU for an
  initial amount of €110 billion

Figure 1.1 Timeline of the Financial Crisis

Government in the eighteenth century taking a vested interest in what were colloquially known as 'monied companies' – the Bank of England, the South Sea Company, and the United East India Company, for example – on the basis of preserving 'confidence in the "public credit"'.[26] Additionally, Benton Gup noted how TBTF policies can take different forms other than cash injections, with it being noted that George W. Bush actively protected the ailing US Steel industry from competition by placing restrictive tariffs on imported steel.[27]

However, whilst all of the above is true, the banking sector provides us with a unique case study. The term 'Too Big to Fail', in the banking sense at least, can be derived from the failure of Continental Illinois in 1984, which was the seventh largest bank in the US at the time of its failure. Stern and Feldman discuss how, at the time, it was considered that the bank's unsecured creditors received 'exceptionally generous government protection'. Citing Congressman Stewart McKinney:

> We have a new kind of bank. And today there is another type created. We found it in the thrift institutions, and now we have given approval for a $1 billion brokerage deal to Financial Corporation America. Mr Chairman, let us not bandy words. We have a new kind of bank. It is called too-big-to-fail, and it is a wonderful bank.[28]

The benefits of a TBTF bank are, theoretically, many. The bank will be able to take advantage of economies of scale, move into profitable markets easier than if it were smaller, and also absorb issues better than their smaller counterparts. However, the concept of TBTF within the banking sphere has been widely and consistently attached to the concept of a 'moral hazard'. Stern and Feldman contest that the 'roots of the TBTF problem lie in creditors' expectations', in that those creditors will come to *expect* that the Government will bail out the bank if needs be. The effect of this is that 'bank creditors who do not face the full cost of the failure of their bank lose some of their incentive to monitor and assess its riskiness'.[29] Sheila C. Bair, the former Chairwoman of the Federal Deposit Insurance Corporation, further argued that 'the reality is there are investors and creditors out there that have relied on "too big to fail" to make investment decisions [and that] we have to take this security blanket away'.[30] This *expectation*, if true, leads to a number of connected issues which result in the concept of a moral hazard, particularly when those issues are internalised by Governments who have the power to take action in favour of the banks. The reason why this is such an issue is simple: Governments must utilise public funds in order to provide such assistance, which draws those same funds away from the public simultaneously. Whilst Governments will eventually claim that their 'quantitative easing' packages result in profitability for the public purse in the long run – as the US announced in 2014[31] – the reality is that the citizenry had to do without those funds in the interim, often during periods of reduced public expenditure across the board.

This interconnectivity between the apparent need to 'bail-out' institutions and utilise the public purse effectively is central to this issue of TBTF. Moosa discusses how the concept of TBTF is rarely mentioned by Governments because of this interconnectedness, whilst he also muses whether the reality is that it is more a case of 'too-*public*-to-fail', rather than too-big-to-fail.[32] This makes sense, in that if the Government is to use public funds to bail out *private* institutions, then it is easier for the public to tolerate if the institutions are clearly visible and have a deemed public importance. It is this dynamic that leads onlookers to describe a 'wealth transfer', in that the Financial Crisis demonstrated 'an immediate wealth transfer from the public to the financial [sector]. Further, the financial institution[s] would have also transferred all the risk of the volatile assets from its balance sheet to the public'.[33] Paul Krugman, in the wake of the Crisis and as the TARP (Troubled Assets Relief Programme[34]) and its *actual* effect came to view, remarked 'what possible justification can there be for doing this without an equity stake? No equity stake, no deal'.[35] Interestingly, other Governments did take an equity stake in the banks that they bailed out, with the British Government and RBS being a prime example, although the first sale of a tranche of shares resulted in a massive £1.07 billion loss,[36] whilst the second sale in 2018 resulted in a £2.1 billion loss.[37]

The actual dynamics of TBTF are what lead to inefficiency and wastage, as demonstrated by the British Government's handling of RBS during and after the Crisis. Stern and Feldman suggest that it is the expectation of TBTF coverage that leads to a reduction in the welfare of the citizenry,[38] and the impact of austerity upon society may be seen as their understanding being correct.[39] Yet, the dynamics of TBTF are interestingly conflicting. At the time of writing, the US has a Republican Administration, and in the UK there is a Conservative Government. These parties are the bastions of free-markets and laissez-faire capitalism, but in reality, their Democratic/Labour counterparts, at least in recent times, have also signed up to the same free-market principles.[40] It is therefore interesting that these governments have, almost successively, championed free-market principles whilst never demonstrating them in reality. Free-market, or laissez-faire capitalism, dictates that 'firms must be left to bear the discipline for failures meted out by the market forces'.[41] However, it is clear that large financial and nonfinancial institutions are being shielded from this market discipline by Government. There is a question of whether this is done selectively, or whether it is an inherent characteristic of TBTF.

Moosa asks whether the Financial Crisis demonstrated that the reality is actually 'too politically connected to fail'.[42] This is based on a narrative that suggested that AIG was saved by the US Government whilst Lehman Brothers was allowed to fail, mostly because if AIG would have collapsed it would have taken Goldman Sachs with it – the Treasury Secretary at the time, Hank Paulson, was the former CEO at Goldman before joining the Government and was one of many former Goldman employees in top positions within the Government. Other analyses point towards the fact that the TBTF dynamic is rooted within a time inconsistency. Whilst regulators and policymakers really ought to take a long-term approach to their decision-making processes, the pressures inherent within a financial collapse usually lead to a fervent environment characterised by short-termism. The need to protect the larger system from the falling dominoes, and also to be perceived to be taking action to stop wider 'runs' on financial institutions, means that short-term decisions are taken and market forces are constrained. The perverse reality is that whilst market forces would naturally mean that a distressed bank wind up slowly, or at least conservatively on account of a lack of access to further credit, the TBTF process usually injects increased amounts of capital into institutions heading towards insolvency anyway – the circumvention of market forces in that manner fundamentally increases systemic risk.[43]

Perhaps the main question, then, is why save banks at all? The answer is simply because banks are very important. They have been described as 'unique economic entities, primarily due to their ability to create money and the impact that bank information production and liquidity services have on the real economy'.[44] However, this societal role means that there is an 'inherent fragility [in] their business model' and, as such, there is a valid argument that 'even the strongest bank cannot survive a severe loss of confidence'.[45] It is very easy to overplay the importance of banks and just focus on when they transgress, but the reality is that the modern, market-based society is *reliant* on the banks. This is why attempts to move forward past the Crisis have focused on the intermediation and possible ways to *dis*intermediate the system, that is, via cryptocurrencies. The effect of that understanding leads to questions of whether the rescuing of banks is a societal truth that we must just accept. There is an issue with that, however, when as Yesha Yadav tells us, in the US 'equity ownership of the twenty-six largest and most systemic U.S. banks has come to be focused in the hands of five major shareholders [BlackRock; Fidelity; State Street; T. Rowe Price; and Vanguard]'.[46] So, whilst it may be a question of the systemic order, it may also be the reality of the public providing guarantees for a small group of very powerful and influential *private* firms. Yet, it has been noted that bankers themselves view the TBTF concept in the banking sector as being a moral hazard as being 'particularly offensive, often responding as if their integrity has been impugned'.[47] Stern and Feldman state that they do not suggest that bankers scheme to defraud Government and public funds, but that they simply respond to signals from the marketplace, as rational actors. If this is the case, then what were those signals before the Financial Crisis that the bankers responded to?

1.3 Mortgage Lending

As we continue through the story of the Financial Crisis, it will become ever clearer that there was no one cause of the Crisis. There were many constituent parts, and some were more important to the overall system than others. However, in the process of originating and maintaining mortgages on mostly residential properties, we can witness the fuel that allowed this particular vehicle to propel itself along and, ultimately, crash. Whilst the US Senate were focusing on the actions of Washington Mutual, they neatly summed up the issue for us:

> The Subcommittee investigation indicates that unacceptable lending and securitisation practices were not restricted to Washington Mutual, but were present at a host of financial institutions that originated, sold, and securitised billions of dollars in high risk, poor quality home loans that inundated U.S. financial markets. Many of the resulting securities ultimately plummeted in value, leaving banks and investors with huge losses that helped send the economy into a downward spiral . . . the high risk loans they issued were the fuel that ignited the financial crisis.[48]

The simple understanding is that mortgage originators first began selling their mortgages to banks that would securitise thousands of these mortgages. In packaging them together, and with the assistance of the Credit Rating Agencies who would apply their top ratings to the securities in order to be sold around the world to investors, the banks increased the demand for mortgages. As a result, mortgage originators would begin to facilitate mortgages for those who could not afford them, just in order to push them through the machine which meant nobody in the chain would suffer if and when those mortgage-holders defaulted on their loans; it would be the system that would suffer. Eventually, the mortgage holders did begin to default on mass, which in turn left banks and investors around the world holding securities that were worthless. Summing up the mortgage-backed financial crisis in one paragraph is tempting, but is certainly not appropriate. That is because there were a whole host of factors involved and, if we are to learn from the debacle, it is important to gain a deeper understanding.

With regard to how to tell this story, there are two different schools of thought within the literature and we shall address those in turn. The major argument surrounds the concept of *deregulation* and its effects. On one side the argument is that:

> by the mid-1990s, the pieces were in place in a deregulated mortgage market for a wholesale shift from 30-year fixed mortgages to short-term mortgages. Securitisation, largely unregulated mortgage companies driven by executive pay linked to their stock prices, and regulators who did not believe in regulating at the Federal Reserve were all in place.[49]

On the other side of the argument the suggestion is that whilst the issue of sub-prime mortgage regulation is important and clearly a central component to the story of the Crisis, 'it does not follow, however, that we should attribute the crisis to the *deregulation* of subprime lending'.[50] Whilst Friedman and Kraus are certainly not champions of this latter school of thought, they do argue that we need to understand the housing bubble and the financial crisis as two different entities. This viewpoint is based on the tendency to attribute blame to a number of key policy decisions taken in the 1990s that would, as some argue, facilitate the Financial Crisis some years later; Friedman and Kraus are of the opinion that the increased complexity in this, and all financial crises, means that attributing blame to this or that is not helpful.

That may be the case, but there were a number of policy actions taken before the Crisis that deserve our attention. Silvers notes that by 1997 the Federal Reserve, led by Alan Greenspan, had lifted the Gross Revenue Limitation for banks from 5% to 25%. Silvers goes further by suggesting that the decision to allow the Citicorp-Travelers merger was the next step in destroying the relevant sections of the Glass–Steagall Act, an Act which was designed to forbid so-called 'Universal Banking'. He notes that this was interesting, in that Citi had already acquired the Brokerage House that had pioneered private-label mortgage-backed securities. Further still, the passing of the Gramm–Leach–Bliley Act is seen by Silvers as the completion of the deregulatory project that now saw Universal banks have the ability to fully ingratiate themselves into the Mortgage-Backed Securities (MBS) marketplace, which crucially included the ability to partake in 'proprietary trading' – this describes when a bank uses the bank's capital to gain investment returns for the bank itself, rather than its clients.[51] This was not the only deviation from normal practice, because the Banks were also develop-ing certain products that meant the banks would only make money when their clientele lost theirs; essentially, the banks were taking positions against their clients. The Senate investigations concur with Silvers when they declare that the decision of Congress to enact the Commodity Futures Modernisation Act 2000 was the final stage, as federal regulations were from then barred from the trillion-dollar swaps market.

However, there is an opposing school of thought that praises the development of Universal Banking (and the deregulation required to ensure it). Rooted in the works of George J. Benston,[52] the argument goes that financial stability is more likely in a system containing Universal Banks, because those banks are more diversified and can withstand shocks better. Furthermore, any market fail-ure containing Universal Banks would be the fault of Central Banks and their policies, not of the banks themselves. Lastly, a concentration of power and all that comes with that is not a consequence of Universal Banking, nor is a decrease in competition, but would simply be a failure of antitrust laws. This was further developed by Charles Calomiris who argued that, in fact, 'deregulation cush-ioned the financial system's adjustment to the subprime shock by making banks more diversified and by allowing troubled investment banks to become stabilised by becoming, or being acquired by, commercial banks'.[53] In other works, Calomiris has gone further, in one instance, *praising* the allocation of TARP funds as 'surgical' and appropriate.[54] Calomiris' work provided academic substance to the widely dismissed claims of Peter J. Wallison, whose dissent in the Financial Crisis Inquiry Commission's investigation was based upon his reckoning that the GSEs and Governmental policy were squarely to blame. Calomiris further states that:

> Clearly, the claim that 'deregulation' produced the subprime crisis is a false diagnosis. Regulatory failure (especially with respect to the GSEs and prudential banking regulation) was a major contributor of the crisis. But deregulation of branching and bank powers over the past two decades has helped to mitigate the fallout from the crisis in many ways.[55]

That the deregulatory phase was underway is perhaps beyond question, with the main question instead being what the effect of that phase was. Nevertheless, a number of vital components were taking shape, like when in 1994 a JPMorgan employee who had attended a conference from within which the concept of a Credit Default Swap was formed remarked 'I've known people who worked on the Manhattan Project – for those of us on that trip, there was the same kind of feeling of being present at the creation of something incredibly important'.[56] At the same time as this deregulation and financial innovation was taking place, there were a number of policy decisions being taken with regard to housing in the US.

One of the key arguments for the school of thought that pins the blame on Governmental legislation and policy, and not the financial industries connected to the Crisis, is that the enactment of the Community Reinvestment Act of 1977, which was amended in 1995, pushed banks to increase their exposure to what are known as 'non-Traditional Mortgages', or NTMs. In conjunction with this, the enactment of the Housing and Community Development Act of 1992 pushed two key Government-Sponsored Entities (GSEs) – Fannie Mae and Freddie Mac – into aggressively facilitating the extension of mortgage facilities to low- and moderate-income borrowers.[57] The Community Reinvestment Act was designed to rectify issues of racism within mortgage lending within the US (so-called 'redlining'), and in 1995 it was amended so that all Federally-insured banks had to demonstrate that they were attempting to extend credit to people within certain income brackets, or at least not preventing access. It is this criterion that critics have focused on as a governmental policy that forced banks into NTMs. However, Freidman advances, via the Superintendent of Banks for the State of New York, that 'only 6 percent of subprime loans were issued by banks subject to the CRA'. Friedman states that this is because the vast majority of 'sub-prime' mortgages were originated in the 'shadow banking system' by the likes of mortgage specialists such as Countrywide and New Century, rather than commercial and Federally-insured Banks like Wells Fargo and CitiBank.[58] If we can safely dispel that one myth advanced by critics, the next claim is more difficult to counter.

Fannie Mae, or as it is officially known the Federal National Mortgage Association, was formed in 1938 by Congress to repurchase mortgages from commercial banks so that the banks would be able to further extend credit to people who needed it to buy homes. After being pseudo-privatised in 1968 in order to remove the liabilities from the Government's balance sheets, it was joined off-book by the Federal Home Loan Mortgage Corporation, better known as Freddie Mac, in 1970. These two GSEs existed to buy and then securitise mortgages from the commercial sector, in order to allow for banks to refill the capacity the two GSEs would have allowed. In 1995, the Department of Housing and Urban Development (HUD) instructed the two GSEs to supplement the initiatives of the Federal Housing Administration with the aim of providing even more opportunities for home ownership. In response, Fannie Mae introduced an incredibly low 3% down mortgage in 1997, which was a massive deviation from their traditional rates of 20% down – the Loan-to-Value Ratio immediately shot up from 80% to 97%. The implicit governmental backing of the GSEs was seen as the leveller in lending to people who had poor credit scores, although technically neither GSE was permitted to lend to people classified as 'subprime'. Friedman confirms that the term 'subprime' does not apply to the *mortgage*, but the credit score of the borrower. Yet, it is not difficult to comprehend that there is a massive overlap between those classified as 'subprime' and those with low incomes and/ or poor credit scores. Nevertheless, in 2000 HUD pressed the two GSEs further, instructing them to direct more than 50% of their financing towards low-income borrowers. The GSEs then responded with their 'American Dream Commitment' and 'Catch the Dream' initiatives. In the Senate's investigations they conclude that, after 2000, 'the number of high risk loans increased rapidly, from about $125 billion in dollar value . . . to about $1 trillion in dollar value . . . altogether from 2000 to 2007, U.S. lenders originated about 14.5 million high risk loans'.[59] It is clear to see why then critics would focus on the GSEs. Essentially, it appears as if HUD had ordered for the increase in lending irrespective of an understanding of who may need to be approached or advertised to if those targets were to be met. However, according to Friedman, there is a crucial part of the story missing in that evaluation.

In 2006 house prices in the US began to fall. As a result, perhaps based on the negative wealth effect, or even just a general lack in confidence in the economic system, the rate of defaults on mortgages began to rise at the same time. The result was that the solvency of the GSEs, who held large amounts of the defaulting debt, was threatened and action was needed. Even though the governmental safety net was only implicit, it was real when it mattered and in September 2008 the two GSEs were bailed out by the Government for more than £382 billion. The crucial part of the story in Freidman's narrative, however, is that this bailing out of the GSEs merely added to the Country's fiscal debt, which he argues cannot have caused the Crisis of 2008 (it may cause a Crisis in the future, of course). The reason for this is that whilst commercial banks did hold mortgage-backed securities (MBS) that were created by the GSEs, that was not all they held. There is a crucial differentiation in that the MBSs issued by Fannie and Freddie are called *agency bonds*, which distinguishes them from *private label* MBSs, or PLMBSs. So, whilst the GSEs accounted for nearly 40% of all mortgages in the US when the bubble burst, there were more PLMBSs in the system. At the same time, the price of insuring PLMBSs, which is how AIG became so embroiled in the Crisis, rose significantly in early 2007 which is suggested as demonstrating an acknowledged doubt within the marketplace about the safety of these securities. Yet, if the *agency* securities were backed by a GSE and therefore the Government, what were the *private label* securities backed by, given they made up the majority of MBSs in the marketplace? To answer that we must look at a process called *securitisation* and it is here we see the role of the credit rating agencies in all its glory.

1.4 Securitisation

Asset securitisation, as a concept, is a well analysed one.[60] As a result, a simplified explanation of the process is available to us. Essentially, asset securitisation describes when a certain category of loans are pooled together and sold to investors. As a function of those loans – let us say, residential mortgages – the holder of the loan will pay the 'principle payment' and the interest due on the loan in instalments over the lifetime of the loan. That stream of payment, from each loan, is bundled together with the stream of payment from thousands of other loans in the same category, and then the total stream of payment is subdivided. This total stream is divided into 'tranches' – French for 'slices' – and investors then invest in a given tranche of the overall pool. Which tranche an investor invests in will be determined by regulatory constraints, which is in turn determined by a *credit rating* attached to each tranche. The purpose of this concept is to theoretically reduce the risk for investors. Whilst the risk is mitigated by the granularity of the pool, the opposite effect of non-payment of the underlying loans is a collapsing of the pool. In that case, the damage is felt from the ground up, with the 'equity tranches' at the bottom (the home of the lesser-regulated Hedge Funds seeking larger returns) feeling the losses first, whilst the Mezzanine tranches (inhabited by institutions such as Insurers) would be next in line. Finally, the Senior tranche sits at the top of the process, with regulated entities such as Pension Funds required to only invest in Senior tranches, if indeed they chose to do so. Pension Funds, as with the other categories of investors, would invest in securitised products like Collateral Debt Obligations (CDOs) for a number of specific reasons. First, credit rating agencies had to provide ratings to each tranche, with Senior tranches being rated AAA or the equivalent, and the Mezzanine tranche being rated above 'investment grade'; the Equity trance could be classified as below investment grade. As a result, a number of institutions were regulatory constrained to only invest in certain tranches, like Pension Funds being forced to only invest in AAA products on account of their size and connectedness to the public. These institutions would invest in CDOs because (a) they gave better value than investing in corporate bonds of the same rating, and (b) the ratings attached to the products and the tranches were trusted. The common belief was that a AAA rating represented the *fact* that one would be repaid their investment.

However, supposedly unbeknownst to the system at large, there were a number of inherent conflicts within the securitisation process. Investment banks were heavily involved in the whole process, as the Senate report states: 'Investment banks also earned fees from working with the lenders to assemble the pools, design the mortgage backed securities, obtain credit ratings for them, and sell the resulting securities to investors'.[61] However, as was mentioned earlier, the banks had started seeking profit for themselves and not their clientele, and their connections to connected-parties and rule changes – such as the 2002 rule change from the US Treasury that dictated that capital reserves for securitised mortgages could be reduced if they obtained a higher rating – all contributed to the banking system becoming embroiled in the process. It is for this reason that scholars such as Friedman and Krauss question whether the Financial Crisis should be regarded as a *banking crisis* predominantly. The impact of securitisation was stark according to the Senate report:

> The securitisation of higher risk loans led to increased profits, but also injected greater risks into U.S. mortgage markets. Some U.S. lenders, like Washington Mutual and Countrywide, made wholesale shifts in their loan programs, reducing their sale of low risk, 30-year, fixed rate mortgages and increasing their sale of higher risk loans. Because higher risk loans required borrowers to pay higher fees and a higher rate of interest, they produced greater initial profits for lenders than lower risk loans. In addition, Wall Street firms were willing to pay more for the higher risk loans, because once securitised, the AAA securities relying on those loans typically paid investors a higher rate of return that other AAA investments, due to the higher risk involved. As a result, investors were willing to pay more, and mortgage backed securities relying on higher risk loans typically fetched a better price than those relying on lower risk loans. Lenders also incurred little risk from issuing the higher risk loans, since they quickly sold the loans and kept the risk off their books.[62]

It is clear to see that the system was based on a systemic abdication of responsibility. However, there was always a claim that was repeated time and time again, which was that the rating agencies had vouched for the safety of the underlying assets in these securities. Essentially, it should not have mattered whether high-risk loans were being originated and then forced through the securitisation machine because the rating agencies would identify this and then not attach their highest ratings, therefore protecting investors.

I have written about credit rating agencies and their role in the securitisation process before,[63] as have a number of other scholars.[64] So, rather than examine each issue in great depth, we can review the major issues with the credit rating agencies and their role in the Financial Crisis in their essential forms. One of the largest issues is the concept of *reliance*. The leading US-based credit rating agencies are classified by the Securities and Exchange Commission as 'Nationally Recognised Statistical Rating Organisations' (NRSROs) and have been since 1975 (the classification change was initially developed in 1973). The effect of this was that a number of associated regulations mandated that only NRSROs could provide ratings for a given product, which essentially consolidated the position of the credit rating oligopoly. This has led scholars to suggest that what was granted in 1975 was a 'regulatory licence',[65] although other scholars have confirmed that this licensing of the agencies' products has a long history, which has then been labelled as a 'legal licence'.[66] Nevertheless, the effect is the same. Whether through behavioural reasons within the marketplace, or because the agencies are regulatory forced upon the marketplace, investors came to *rely* on the agencies' ratings, either in addition to their own investigations or in lieu of them. The second component of this reliance is bound up in a conflict that dates back to the end of the 1960s – the investors do not pay for the ratings of the largest rating agencies. Since the last 1960s, Moody's, and then S&P 4 years later, have practiced the 'issuer-pays' approach, in which the issuer of the bond or product pays the agency to produce a rating on that given bond or product. So, in relation to the RMBS example, the investment banks who were liaising with mortgage originators, packaging the loans into structured securities, and then selling them to investors were the very same organisations paying the rating agencies to rate those same products.

There is more. Even though the investors were relying on the rating agencies despite not paying them for the ratings, the investors could *theoretically* be forgiven for concluding that the agencies would at least try to be as neutral as possible, mostly on account of preserving their reputation. However, in a particular formula developed to identify a price point, we can witness the mentality of the credit rating agencies in the run-up to the Crisis. The Gaussian Copula Formula is a formula that is used to help quantify the effects of individual elements within a given set of data, for the aim of producing a correlation that can lead to the setting of a price point.[67] The agencies were faced with the issue of having to rate a product that contained thousands of individual products, all of which contained differing levels of risk. As they could not produce a rating on that basis, the Gaussian Copula Formula was an ideal solution. However, there was a crucial issue in that the lack of underlying data had to be filled in order for the Formula to work, and the rating agencies chose to input data from Credit Default Swaps (CDS) and Equity Default Swaps (EDS) premia. This data demonstrates the amount of protection that investors are buying in order to hold RMBSs, which itself is dependent upon credit ratings. This highly procyclical and entirely inappropriate method of calculating risk became an underpinning element of the rating agencies' practice, as it allowed for the development of ratings which were required to send a security through the securitisation machinery. Essentially then, any investors' hope of rating agency neutrality had disappeared, only they did not know it.

Once the bubble began to burst, the credit rating agencies really took centre stage. In producing the US's first period of 'mass-downgrades', the market was obliterated. Investors lost the value of their holdings in an instant, and as a number of entities were now holding securities that they could not hold on account of the regulations (as the rating on the products had dropped below investment grade), the result was that financial entities were left holding entirely worthless and toxic stock. This continued and the Financial Crisis was then in full swing. To add to this, once the Crisis had took hold in Europe, a number of mass downgrades within the Sovereign Bond market led to a massive crisis that saw a number of countries needing urgent financial assistance just to stay afloat. It was truly the era of the credit rating agencies.

It is for this reason that this book exists. Whilst many scholars and interested people were aware of the credit rating agencies before the Crisis, their actions in the lead-up, during, and after the Crisis made the leading credit rating agencies part of the societal psyche. This is confirmed further by the enactment of regulations and legislation around the world designed to constrain the activities of the agencies and regulate the impact of the agencies upon economies. Yet, despite a very small blip and also despite receiving record financial penalties for their conduct, the leading agencies have gone from strength to strength, increasing their financial performance and establishing a stronger foothold in the marketplace as a result. So, whilst S&P and Fitch are private companies that do not disclose their data (for the most part), Moody's is a publicly-limited company and, as a result, must publicly publish its data. We therefore have the opportunity to understand one of the major credit rating agencies in fine detail. In this introduction, we have looked at the Financial Crisis and the agencies' role in it, and that is why we must conduct that investigation. Our aim is to *know* Moody's by the end of this book, and by starting from the very beginning and working our way through, we shall do exactly that.

Notes

1 Lawrence J White, 'Credit-Rating Agencies and the Financial Crisis: Less Regulation of CRAs Is a Better Response' (2010) 25(4) Journal of International Banking Law and Regulation 170.
2 Thomas L Friedman, 'Foreign Affairs; Don't Mess with Moody's' *New York Times* (22 February 1995).

3 Moody's, 'Moody's Reaches Settlement with U.S. Department of Justice, 21 States and District of Columbia' *Justice News* (2017).

4 Stephanie Decker, Matthias Kippling and R Daniel Wadhwani, 'New Business Histories! Plurality in Business History Research Methods' (2015) 57(1) Business History 31.

5 ibid 32.

6 Robert T Plant, *Ecommerce: Formulation of Strategy* (Prentice Hall 2000) 72; Arthur V Hill, *The Encyclopedia of Operations Management: A Field Manual and Glossary of Operations Management Terms and Concepts* (FT Press 2012) 16.

7 John W Mayer and Brian Rowan, 'Institutional Organisations: Formal Structure as Myth and Ceremony' in Walter W Powell and Paul J DiMaggio (eds), *The New Institutionalism in Organisational Analysis* (Chicago UP 2012) 22.

8 Tara Rooney, Katrina Lawlor and Eddie Rohan, 'Telling Stories: Storytelling as a Methodological Approach in Research' (2016) 14(2) The Electronic Journal of Business Research Methods 147.

9 ibid 148.

10 Yipeng Liu, Yijun Xing and Mark Starik, 'Storytelling as Research Method: A West-Meets-East Perspective' in Catherine L Wang, David J Ketchen and Donald D Bergh (eds), *West Meets East: Building Theoretical Bridges* (Emerald Group Publishing 2012) 145.

11 Tom Huddleston, 'These 7 Movies Tell the Real Story Behind the Financial Crisis' (2015) *Fortune* (27 December 2015).

12 Daniel Cash, *Regulation and the Credit Rating Agencies: Restraining Ancillary Services* (Routledge 2018) 159.

13 For an excellent examination of the Crisis through a white-collar criminological perspective, see Nicholas Ryder, *The Financial Crisis and White Collar Crime: The Perfect Storm?* (Edward Elgar Publishing 2014).

14 Imad A Moosa and Vikash Ramiah, *The Financial Consequences of Behavioural Biases: An Analysis of Bias in Corporate Finance and Financial Planning* (Springer 2017).

15 Nicholas Ryder, Umut Turksen and Sabine Hassler, *Fighting Financial Crime in the Global Economic Crisis* (Routledge 2014).

16 Prasanta Ray, *The Sociology of Greed: Runs and Ruins in Banking Crises* (Routledge 2018).

17 Kate Power, Tanweer Ali and Eva Lebduskova, *Discourse Analysis and Austerity: Critical Studies from Economics and Linguistics* (Routledge 2019).

18 United States Senate, *Wall Street and the Financial Crisis: Anatomy of a Financial Collapse* (GPO 2011).

19 The table is comprised of data gathered from United States Senate (n 18) 47; Peter Kingsley, 'Financial Crisis: Timeline' *The Guardian* (7 August 2012).

20 Vikas Bajaj, 'Financial Crisis Enters New Phase' *New York Times* (17 September 2008).

21 Nicole Gelinas, 'It's Time to End "Too Big to Fail"' *New York Post* (16 August 2009).

22 Niall Ferguson, 'There's No Such Thing as Too Big to Fail in a Free Market' *The Telegraph* (5 October 2009).

23 United States Senate (n 18) 17.

24 Charles G Leathers and J Patrick Raines, 'Some Historical Perspectives on "Too Big to Fail" Policies' in Benton E Gup (ed), *Too Big to Fail: Policies and Practices in Government Bailouts* (ABC-CLIO 2003).

25 Reuters, 'TIMELINE: Auto Industry in Crisis' *Reuters* (1 May 2009).

26 Leathers and Raines (n 24) 5.

27 Benton E Gup, 'What Does Too Big to Fail Mean?' in Benton E Gup (ed), *Too Big to Fail: Policies and Practices in Government Bailouts* (ABC-CLIO 2003) 29.
28 Gary H Stern and Ron J Feldman, *Too Big to Fail: The Hazards of Bank Bailouts* (Brookings Institution Press 2004) 13.
29 ibid 17.
30 Eric Dash, 'If It's Too Big to Fail, Is It Too Big to Exist' *New York Times* (20 June 2009).
31 Chris Isidore, 'U.S. Ends TARP with $15.3 Billion Profit' *CNN* (19 December 2014).
32 Imad A Moosa, *The Myth of Too Big to Fail* (Springer 2010) 1.
33 Robert W Kolb, *The Financial Crisis of Our Time* (OUP 2011) 133.
34 Timothy G Massad (ed), *Troubled Asset Relief Program (TARP): Two Year Retrospective* (DIANE Publishing 2011).
35 ibid.
36 BBC, 'RBS: Government Sells £2.1bn of Shares in Bank at a Loss' *BBC* (4 August 2015).
37 BBC, 'Government Loses £2.1bn on RBS Stake Sale' *BBC* (5 June 2018).
38 Stern and Feldman (n 28) 23.
39 David Clark, *The Global Financial Crisis and Austerity: A Basic Introduction* (Policy Press 2015).
40 Leathers and Raines (n 24) 3.
41 ibid.
42 Moosa (n 32) 5.
43 Stern and Feldman (n 28) 25.
44 Moosa (n 32) 11.
45 ibid.
46 Yesha Yadav, 'Too-Big-to-Fail Shareholders' (2018) 103(2) Minnesota Law Review 592.
47 Stern and Feldman (n 28) 18.
48 United States Senate (n 18) 4.
49 Damon Silvers, 'Deregulation and the New Financial Architecture' in Martin H Wolfson and Gerald A Epstein (eds), *The Handbook of the Political Economy of Financial Crises* (OUP 2013) 439.
50 Jeffrey Friedman and Wladimir Kraus, *Engineering the Financial Crisis: Systemic Risk and the Failure of Regulation* (Pennsylvania UP 2011) 25.
51 United States Senate (n 18) 17.
52 George J Benston, *The Separation of Commercial and Investment Banking: The Glass-Steagall Act Revisited and Reconsidered* (Palgrave Macmillan 1990) 212.
53 Charles W Calomiris, 'Origins of the Subprime Crisis' in Asli Demirgüç-Kunt and others (eds), *The International Financial Crisis: Have the Rules of Finance Changed?* (World Scientific 2011) 88.
54 Charles W Calomiris, 'The Subprime Turmoil: What's Old, What's New, and What's Next' [2009] Journal of Structured Finance 7.
55 ibid 32.
56 John G Glenn, *Foucault and Post-Financial Crises* (Springer 2018) 3.
57 Peter J Wallison, 'Dissenting Statement' in Phil Angelides (ed), *Financial Crisis Inquiry Report* (DIANE Publishing 2011) 451–5.
58 Jeffrey Friedman, 'Capitalism and the Crisis: Bankers, Bonuses, Ideology, and Ignorance' in Jeffrey Freidman (ed), *What Caused the Financial Crisis* (Pennsylvania UP 2011) 3.
59 United States Senate (n 18) 20.
60 John Deacon, *Global Securitisation and CDOs* (John Wiley & Sons 2004); Vinod Kothari, *Securitisation: The Financial Instrument of the Future* (John Wiley & Sons 2006).

61 United States Senate (n 18) 18.

62 ibid 20.

63 Cash (n 12).

64 Herwig P Langohr and Patricia T Langohr, *The Rating Agencies and Their Credit Ratings: What They Are, How They Work, and Why They Are Relevant* (John Wiley & Sons 2010).

65 Frank Partnoy, 'The Siskel and Ebert of Financial Markets? Two Thumbs Down for the Credit Rating Agencies' (1999) 77 Washington University Law Quarterly 3.

66 Marc Flandreau and Joanna K Sławatyniec, 'Understanding Rating Addiction: US Courts and the Origins of Rating Agencies' Regulatory Licence (1900–1940)' (2013) 20 Financial History Review 3.

67 Joseph P Farrell, *Babylon's Banksters: The Alchemy of Deep Physics, High Finance and Ancient Religion* (Feral House 2010) 21–7.

2 The Long Road Home Must Start Somewhere

2.1 Introduction

In the foreword to his 1933 autobiography *A Long Road Home*, John Moody, the founder of Moody's, begins with the following question: 'Why should I, a man of no importance outside my little world, indulge in such insufferable conceit as to write a story about myself, and flaunt it before the public?'[1] Ninety years on at the time of writing, this book perhaps exists as the answer to that humble question. In relation to his own autobiography, Moody continued by saying that:

> Now, J.M. Barrie has said that 'The Life of a man is a diary in which he means to write one thing and writes another'. And in trying to see in retrospect the crowded years of a life which has reached its afternoon, one's perspective of past events may be distorted; though usually at a distance it may be seen how these events are interwoven, and thus their meaning better understood.

This thinking has been instructive to me as an author. Whilst it may indeed be the case that aspects are lost to history as time progresses, or captured in a manner that does not represent the truth of the time, the interweaving of developments is something that this book aims to achieve in bringing the Moody's story to life. However, where does one start? Would it be interesting to you, the reader, to start with the birth of a young John Moody in New Jersey, three years after the US Civil War ended and continue from there?[2] Perhaps. Yet, when I delved into the world of credit ratings, I wanted to learn more about the start of the idea of rating in the financial sector, in the truest sense of the word. In the literature, the world of credit ratings starts with John Moody in 1900 and nothing comes before it, but is it really the case that the idea of rating entities started as last as 1900? The British Empire that birthed the Industrial Revolution was founded on extraordinary levels of trade, and the American era that it facilitated is intrinsically connected to the concept of entrepreneurism and expansive trade. Surely then, the young John Moody would have been influenced to develop the 'first rating agency' in 1900?

DOI: 10.4324/9781003001065-2

Unsurprisingly, that is indeed the case. Whilst it is tempting to fall in line with the majority of the literature that neatly defines the credit rating agencies away from any associated attempts to conduct surveillance on financial entities, one can only truly understand the *character* of somebody or something by understanding what may have impacted them, influenced them, or inspired them. John Moody's story is an interconnected story that has ties to Benjamin Franklin, major milestones in the abolition of slavery in the US, and an intrinsic connection to a foundational period in modern America's history. Starting that story in 1900 fundamentally restricts our understanding of the man, his ideas, his vision, and ultimately his impact upon society. I, for one, am glad that he chose to 'indulge in such insufferable conceit'.

The chapter therefore may seem abstract to some. It will veer from Victorian Britain to the industrial expansion of the globally influential island, from the antebellum 'United Colonies' to the expansion of the railroads. It will contain characters that dominated the era and upstarts who dared to challenge the establishment with innovative and era-defining ideas. It will portray a story of technological developments that survive to this day, and it will ultimately reveal a systemic reality that is as important today as it was almost 200 years ago. We will start by learning more about reasons why creditworthiness assessments were necessary, and the earliest efforts to meet that need. From that point, the chapter will analyse the first commercial attempts at providing creditworthiness assessments on a broad, industrial scale. Those efforts were ultimately successful after a first failed foray and grew into a substantial and solidified industry that gave the young John Moody inspiration (including from within his extended family that connected the two industries).

2.2 Creditworthiness as a Concept and the Birth of the Agency

At its core, the concept of trade is inseparable from the concept of trust. This relationship is only heightened with the addition of credit. A handful of researchers have endeavoured to examine the relatively modern genealogy of credit-based infrastructures and that research has led to eighteenth-century Britain, within which traders were faced with a clear problem: how does one guard against fraud, fraudsters, and essentially those who cannot or should not be trusted to trade with or extend credit to? Their answer was to form 'Trade Protection Societies' which brought together businesspeople within particular regions to centralise information on people's reputation, trading history, and likely capacity to meet obligations. The Societies were created to 'balance competition with cooperation, as well as creating, policing, and enforcing trust'.[3] The Societies were based on two initiatives. The first was the development of local Courts of Requests (or Recovery) that were established via private Acts of parliament, and which provided redress for small debts and other financial claims. These courts had the effect of discouraging defaults. The second initiative that was developed in line with the Courts of Requests from the establishment of private local societies to prosecute 'felons and swindlers'. The 1770s have been identified as a starting point for each of these initiatives and they would provide a clear template for the Trade Protection Societies that would seek to merge the capabilities of the initiatives towards the end of the eighteenth century. The UK would seek to formalise the Courts of Recovery in the early nineteenth century with the establishment of 'County Courts', although they were deemed to be too sympathetic to those who failed to meet their obligations, and their outcomes too unpredictable. In response, there was a rapid growth of Trade Protection Societies that sought to provide information for members on businesspeople so that they could be better informed about the chances of their trading partners meeting their obligations.[4]

At the same time, the large British financiers of the time were seeking to take advantage of the expansion of the Americas. However, the financiers were exposed to a problem of the time: the lack of technology to help overcome the many difficulties associated with trading across thousands of miles. As Hidy explains: 'During the years after the Napoleonic Wars merchant bankers, including Baring Brothers and Company, faced new complexities in the management of their business. Among the new problems was to find a satisfactory means of selecting trustworthy correspondents'.[5] At the same time, other leading European-based financiers, like Salomon de Rothschild, were seeking to do business in the expanding Americas but were met with hostility and, as such, there was an additional need to understand more about what was becoming an increasingly hostile trading environment for foreign financiers.[6] To resolve this issue, Thomas Baring, son of the Founder of Baring Brothers Sir Francis (with John Baring being a founding silent partner), looked to capitalise on his company's position in the US after facilitating the Louisiana Purchase.[7] However, to navigate the difficulties above he turned to a trusted correspondent from Boston – Thomas Wren Ward – who would, based on his years of experience, devise a network of informants and systematically gather information on businesspeople across the eastern Seaboard to be sent to his London-based paymasters.

The Barings understood that their successes in the Americas relied solely upon the strength and quality of the informational networks they would utilise; they were to be dealing with a changing array of people in a land they did not know. So, during a tour of the US in 1829, Thomas Baring signed a contract with Ward (whom he met via a personal connection) to the effect of making Ward a 'Special Resident Agent' of Baring Brothers in North America. Baring also signed similar deals in other regions of the country – like with Edmond J. Forstall in New Orleans – to bolster his continental presence.[8] Ward would establish a 'very effective' system of categorising the credit potential of entities in his region and send correspondence to London at regular intervals; by 1831 the system was well underway and the itemisation including information on the location of the firm in question, its capital, particular preoccupation, its character, the amount of credit Ward thought was safe to extend, conditions under which such credit should be extended, and another other relevant information Ward saw fit to include. To make things even more convenient for the Baring Brothers management structure, Ward placed each firm into a sliding scale, ranging from: 'may be considered as Houses not only entirely safe for what they may do, but likely to continue so under any possible circumstances', to 'No trust: This column consists of those who either have no capital or are not of the character to render it desirable to trust them at all'.[9]

It is clear to see that what Ward developed, essentially, is the investment-grade and non-investment-grade demarcations. On one side of the Atlantic there were financiers developing sophisticated networks of information via informants and on the other there were Trade Protection Societies centralising the collection of information on the creditworthiness of businesspeople. It stands to reason then that one of these approaches would have simply been extended to the Americas, but there are relative applicability issues with both. Olegario notes that the Trade Protection Societies would not have worked in the much larger and therefore much more transient American business environment,[10] whilst alternatively, Madison discusses how the reports garnered via the financiers' networks were 'high in quality, but they were also high in cost'.[11] What was needed then was an entity that could provide the level of rich information that would be needed but in a manner where the cost was affordable. The way in which this would be achieved would be to commercialise the process. It has been noted that attempts were made to do this in 1810 in England with a firm called Perry's, but little is known of that endeavour and, irrespective, it did not last long.[12] In the US, it would be twenty five years later that the first attempt at commercialisation would be made, with a New York City Law Firm called Griffen, Cleaveland, and Campbell developing a 'comprehensive plan' for credit reporting in 1835.[13] The firm established a network of lawyers around the city to:

> provide regular evaluations of local businesses that bought their stock in New York City. After paying an annual subscription fee, any merchant in New York could consult these reports as often as he wished. The reporting attorneys received fees for their work, as well as the prospect of additional retainers, since Griffen, Cleaveland, and Campbell promised to forward any requests for collection of outstanding debt.

However, in a theme that would and continues to repeat throughout the ages within the connected industries, an agency's success is mostly determined by their environment. The Law Firm started the rating process in 1835, at the time of a 'heady economic boom': 'the heady economic boom of the mid-1830s reduced the caution of many merchants, and hence their willingness to pay for information about the economic prospects of potential customers'. In addition, one of the partners of the firm had suffered substantial losses from real-estate speculations and this placed an insufferable pressure on the law firm.[14] In that vacuum, Balleisen remarks that:

> By 1841, however, the well-known merchant, philanthropist, and abolitionist Lewis Tappan had resolved to make a second attempt to develop a credit-reporting agency, drawing heavily on the earlier scheme of Griffen, Cleaveland, & Campbell. Tappan enjoyed better timing than the three lawyers. He began the Mercantile Agency after the economic revulsions of the late 1830s and early 1840s, which reminded businessmen throughout the country that the credit system presented great dangers as well as great opportunities.[15]

We shall meet Lewis Tappan next, but there are elements of the real story which will show us that historical accounts are layered with traps and misconceptions which, although entirely innocent, do not allow for the target of the research to be understood properly (there may be some in this account of course, as no historical investigation can be absolutely accurate or fully inclusive of all the available information).

Lewis Tappan, born in Northampton, Massachusetts in 1788, is a critical part of the US's story, for a number of reasons. Part of a family of eleven siblings (nine survived childhood), Lewis can count four of his siblings who would go on to become 'well-known' in the US, including his brother Benjamin who would become a Senator, John and Charles who would become very successful Bostonian merchants, and Arthur who Lewis would move to New York with to find their fortunes.[16] Tappan was also the great-grandnephew of Benjamin Franklin.[17] There is little known about the young Lewis, except that he was part of a devout Christian family, was regarded as a skilled orator at a young age, but that even though his elder brother Benjamin wanted to take Lewis to Ohio to train as a lawyer, Tappans' mother forbade the idea, as Lewis 'avowed loose sentiments on religious matters'. It is often strongly intimated that Tappan's family engrained within him his evangelical beliefs that would later become a major part of his life,[18] but this is not accurate. Instead, the 15-year-old Lewis would head to Boston with his elder brothers to work for the firm of Benjamin and Timothy, who were importing British goods. He quickly moved on from menial tasks to maintaining the books for the company, and only a small number of years later was worth $50,000 (in 1823). He said at the time: 'I am too much engrossed in business, not my own so much as others'. Interestingly, Tappan would try to form a number of Partnerships in a short amount of time. He wrote under a pseudonym about the benefits of Savings Banks for labourers, so much so that he and twenty others developed the first New England bank of the sort – the Provident Institution for Savings – as well as serving as a treasurer and trustee at a local school that adopted his idea of incorporating a similar practice to 'the Lancastrian System of Instruction' that took the form of using monitors as a mode of mutual instruction within the schooling system.[19] These themes of collaborating for others, entrepreneurship, and affecting educational policies would define the life of Tappan.

After suffering from debt-related difficulties in Boston,[20] Lewis moved to New York City at the invitation of his brother, Arthur. Lewis, in taking the reins, quickly positioned Arthur Tappan and Company as one of the leading mercantile companies in the City, with revenues well in excess of a million dollars. It has been said that, interestingly:

> Lewis Tappan attributed the firm's success to various factors, one of them being the policy of cash sales. Contrary to accepted practices, the company avoided the credit system (except on a short-term basis) and sold goods for cash, at a single, low price.[21]

Tappan's view on the concept of credit was affirmed by Olegario who noted that 'Tappan outdid many Jacksonians in his stated dislike of credit'.[22] Furthermore, and away from his business ventures, Tappan was renowned for his commitment to causes that meant a great deal to him – although, as we shall come to know, there was often a difference between the public and private persona of the man. For example, 'not only did Tappan support the end of slavery, but he also supported racial integration as a logical result of abolishing slavery'[23] and worked actively on creating multi-racial schools and persevered despite being publicly attacked for doing so.[24] Perhaps one of the most public elements of Tappan's legacy, aside from the Mercantile Agency he would create, was his involvement in the infamous *La Amistad* case involving rebellious slaves on board the eponymous schooner that was transporting the slaves at the time. For two years from the time of the arrest of fifty-four Africans on board in 1836, Tappan 'was responsible for their obtaining spiritual guidance, an interpreter, and legal counsel; he worked with the case until the final decision by the Supreme Court in 1841 that freed the Africans'.[25] Yet, whilst Tappan's piousness led him to be involved in a number of ground-breaking developments and initiatives, the reality is that 'when it mattered, Tappan was seldom sentimental'[26] and that, ultimately, Tappan possessed a 'streak of unpleasant opportunism when circumstances allowed'.[27] We may find evidence of this in the fact that, despite his endeavours, 'the Tappans never employed blacks as their clerks in their wholesaling business, even when urged by a black minister to do so'[28] or that, towards the end of his life, he actively worked with pro-slavery people from the South of the US in order to continue financial successes. But, the origins of the Mercantile Agency provide a gleaming exhibit of the reality of Lewis Tappan.

First, let us obtain some context. In 1835, the law firm of Griffen, Cleaveland, & Campbell had attempted to start the first commercial reference agency. Though Tappan did not like using credit, a number of his suppliers did and, after a number of suppliers reneged on their obligations in 1837 because of the volatile marketplace that existed in the antebellum US (due to its relative infancy), Arthur Tappan and Company would default on their own obligations. This million-dollar enterprise's collapse shocked the City of New York and 'helped spark the Panic of 1837'.[29] The ensuing financial crisis that engulfed the country at the time led, just four years later, to the enacting of The National Bankruptcy Act of 1841 which, amongst its many facets, appeared to favour the idea of debtors being able to be pardoned for their debts. The result, naturally, was that 'creditors feared a "Jubilee": in the Book of Leviticus, the universal pardoning of debts'. Meanwhile, Tappan had purchased the subscriber base of Griffen, Cleaveland & Campbell[30] after it had failed in 1837 and literally a few days before the National Bankruptcy Act of 1841 was enacted, Tappan officially launched the Mercantile Agency.[31] It mattered not that Congress repealed the Law just months later because of the public backlash, or that it was Tappan's company that had ignited the flames of the financial crisis of the time – Tappan was now in business and had capitalised, fully, on the fear of the time.

The Mercantile Agency represented something new for the world. As Sandage describes:

> When Tappan began in 1841, no comparable system of surveillance had ever existed. Within five years, he enlisted 679 local informants; after ten, his network reached 2,000. Their first decade of dispatches filled 'more than 100 books, of the size of the largest ledger, extending to 600 and 700 pages each'. One 11-by-17-inch page held up to 1,500 words of tiny calligraphy, the handiwork of 'a great many clerks'. By 1851, the inflow kept thirty scriveners busy. Indexing within and among volumes sped retrieval of any given entry among thousands and later millions. Cross-referencing aided continuous tracking, even when subjects changed pursuits or locales . . . the agency upgraded the most adaptable and dependable technology in human history – the book – by building networks and systems around it.[32]

Tappan had learned something from his analysis of the marketplace and the attempts of Griffen, Cleaveland & Campbell in that 'he came to see the credit-reporting business as potentially immune from the vagaries of the business cycle'. So much so, he would write that 'in prosperous times [subscribers] will feel able to pay for the information and in bad times they feel they must have it'.[33] The cycle-busting business would become central to an industry that would lead the way for the early American economy. To overcome some of the core issues that were affecting the early company, Tappan pioneered the private usage of the branch structure that is commonplace in modern business practice. Opening first in Boston in 1843, the Mercantile Agency would go on to have branches in Philadelphia, Baltimore, Cincinnati, before Tappan's successors went on to greatly increase the influence and spread of the business.[34] Furthermore, the company became early adopters of innovative technology like typewriters and telegraphs. The spread of the agency allowed Tappan to achieve his aim of 'purifying the mercantile air'.

To achieve this aim, Tappan developed a particular process. Wyatt-Brown describes how Tappan organised a vast network of 'correspondents' – one of who was Abraham Lincoln prior to his Presidency[35] – who would send in reports twice a year (on February and August 1st) 'in time for the fall and spring sales when inland storekeepers descended on New York like a swarm of transient birds'. Interestingly, he continues by detailing how:

> the reporter's only compensation came from collection cases. Whenever a delinquency occurred, the subscriber was supposed to notify Tappan, who then referred him to the appropriate correspondent. The attorney would then receive notice to prosecute, obtaining a commission fee out of whatever amount he could extract from the defaulting storekeepers. His reports to Tappan, therefore, brought him no immediate return, only the prospect of business from the New York subscribers.[36]

In terms of where the correspondents got their information, each would have a range of 'informants' who would be protected by the Agency who would use code numbers to mask the identity of the underlying informants.[37] It is not surprising then that the Agency came in for extensive criticism.

Wyatt-Brown writes that 'Tappan regarded his "correspondents" more as sentinels than snitches'[38] and this makes sense, given his predilection for 'cleansing' the marketplace. However, this view was not shared by many. Others rather saw the agency as 'an organised system of espionage, which, centred in New York, extends its ramifications to every city, village, and school district in the Union'.[39] A leading newspaper editor of the day denounced the Agency as a 'new clap-trap for notoriety . . . carrying on the business of a secret inquiry into private affairs and personal standing of everybody buying goods in New York'.[40] The contrasting views ranged from the Agency as developing social control and discipline via surveillance, to what the New York Office of Brown Brothers wrote in 1858, that the Agency 'pursues business for gain and may not care where the information comes from'.[41] The focus on the source and quality of information is interesting, because as Phillips suggests, the ratings books were 'inadequate and not always in accord with the facts',[42] 'shortcomings' that Madison affirms.[43] Others, as well as those paid by the Agency, argued differently, that the Agency provided 'accurate and impartial information',[44] and that the agency's financial successes were a testament as to their usefulness.

Information, and how it is used, is fundamentally intertwined with the fortunes of modern credit rating agencies. The same was true for the first agency, too. During the first few decades of the Agency, the marketplace came to realise that there were a number of issues coming from the new service and began to provide opposition accordingly. That opposition came from several angles but, as we shall see throughout the book, the rating (and reference) industry always had an answer. For example, the opaque nature of the process for the Mercantile Agency (which we shall expand upon next) led to libel charges from businesspeople given poor or, what they argued were inaccurate ratings. To defend against this, the Agency began to encourage businesses to sign and attest to financial statements about their business, which led to an increased quality of information in the system, but also a layer of protection for the Agency, especially after the 1880s when the courts declared that a business could be held liable for furnishing false information to credit reporters (bringing it in line with the auditing industry).[45]

The courts provided further protection for the industry, although it was for a long time a strained relationship. It has often been proposed in the literature that the judiciary had been favourable to the early machinations of the rating industry, but research has shown this to be untrue. In fact, the courts were quite damning of the early reporting agencies and how they went about their business. One of the key issues was whether a report generated by the Agency could be classified as 'privileged communication', which very simply means communication between parties which the law recognises as a protected relationship. The Agency was arguing that the communication between it and its correspondent, irrespective of whether it was about another person, was 'privileged', just like a conversation between a lawyer and their client. The issue was debated up until 1898, but the issues were important ones. For example, could the information be privileged if it was wrong, or slanderous? There are plenty of evidenced occasions where respondents would maliciously slander rivals via their reports to ruin them, or where the Agency would either negatively rate to punish or positively rate to reward.[46] In fact, the courts ruled overwhelmingly that only one of the four products that the Agency sold – the confidential report – could qualify as privileged communication.[47] The courts placed a heavy emphasis on the need for the Agency to be making communication 'in good faith' and, if they did, the chances of a libel case succeeding became very low indeed.

The courts would continue to have their moment of defiance, like when a Philadelphia-based judge said of the Agency:

> its operations are secret, everything is sent out under the garb of confidence, and thus the poisoned arrows which are launched in darkness, may strike down the purest and most solvent in the land; no businessman is safe, if this can be recognised and protected by law as a privileged communication.

Yet, it would not matter. In 1882 the Federal Courts ruled that credit reports were privileged, and in 1896 gave the Agencies copyright protection. As Sandage concluded, 'the law defined information as the property of the seller, not the buyer or the subject of the report'.[48]

Yet, it was not only the courts that had their crosshairs trained on the burgeoning industry. During the mid-1870s, four States in particular turned their attention to the nascent industry, which at that point had gained its second entrant: Bradstreet Co. In New York, Missouri, Illinois, and Pennsylvania, lawmakers had introduced bills that made the agencies responsible for losses suffered by businesses and businesspeople as a result of inaccurate reports. It is debated whether this was because of the slowly turning tide in the judicial arena towards the agencies, or just from pressure from influential constituents. Nevertheless, three of the bills died early in the process, but in Pennsylvania, the bill ascended and was called 'An Act to Punish Commercial Agents for False Representations of the Business Condition of Certain Persons'. Interestingly, the Agency devoted considerable resources to countering this threat to their existence and undertook a concerted campaign to rally support from influential businesspeople in the Pennsylvania districts, ultimately concluding with the effect of:

> The Senators were fairly overwhelmed with protests against the measure from the biggest men among their constituents in all parts of the State . . . never before had they received so many dispatches, on one subject, from quarters so influential in such a short time . . . this circumstance simply shows what can be done by a little forethought, manipulation, and management in the shape of working-up sentiment in the interest of fair play.[49]

However, in addition to this Flandreau and Mesevage explain how 'the agencies circulated a petition and induced businesses they rated to sign a petition "on the promises of *special* recognition from the Agency" (meaning they would be rewarded through higher ratings)'. There is also evidence of the Agency threatening entities with lower ratings if support for the Agency was not forthcoming.[50] The failure of the legislative bodies and judicial bodies to restrain the industry led to many incidents whereby the Agency crushed prospective litigants with extreme prejudice, to the point where challenges became very few and far between (see the case of *Beardsley v. Tappan* for an excellent example).

For all of the defences given by the Agency and its leaders, the reality became that the Agency 'was a panopticon without walls'.[51] Madison describes this critical era for the development of the nascent industry neatly:

> The extent of this success and the secure place that the once-novel enterprises had won in the American business community were clearly demonstrated by the nature and results of legal, political, and economic attacks directed against the agencies in the late nineteenth century. The attacks took the form of legal suits, attempts to pass regulatory legislation, and efforts to develop new kinds of competition, in all three areas, the established agencies emerged victorious.[52]

Emerge victorious they would do indeed. At the turn of the twentieth century, the credit *reporting* industry was in full swing. John Bradstreet's eponymous reporting agency, created in 1849, would not experience the same growth as the Mercantile Agency until the development of 'the world's first commercial ratings book' in 1857, which revolutionised the concept of the reporting industry and developed the founding tenets of the credit *rating* industry to come.[53] Lewis Tappan would pass the reins of the Mercantile Agency to Robert G. Dun, who would take the Mercantile Agency to new heights. Tappan, upon reflection, would state that one of the biggest regrets of his life was not starting the Mercantile Agency sooner as he enjoyed the fruits of his labour in retirement. However, it was not without hardship, as Tappan would have to jettison his principles to grow the Agency and deal with avowed pro-slavery businessmen (like R.G. Dun), something which he struggled to deal with in his later years.

Nevertheless, the long road that a young John Moody was about to begin had already been started. Quite apart from the accepted literature, the truth is that Moody was about to tap into a long lineage of business surveillance and analysis that had taken a number of forms that were relevant to their environment. Further emphasising the linkages between the two industries – which would be formalised later in the 1960s – Henry Poor of Standard & Poor's fame married Tappan's niece before starting his own business, and John would model his company on the Mercantile Agency (and R.G. Dun and Co.) and Bradstreet Co.'s methods.[54] The early credit rating industry would come to encapsulate the best that the reporting industry had to offer and modify its output for the growing world of securitisation, as well as a growing corporate environment.[55] However, it would also continue intrinsic flaws that, when understood from a wider perspective, perhaps represent the personification of underlying human frailties, that is, greed, insecurity, fear, manipulation, and an absence of moralistic judgement.

In order to understand that genealogy more, we must now meet John Moody. The founder of the company that this book has chosen to focus on, he represents for us a critical subject that we must seek to understand from a variety of angles. His foundations and his character can help illustrate his reasoning, his approaches, and his actions. Despite his humility when reflecting upon his own impact on the world in his retirement, John Moody would become indelibly linked to an industry that would go on to become truly central to modern human existence. In that vein, learning more about the man and the company he created is a worthwhile endeavour and one that we shall begin now.

2.3 John Moody

The story of Moody's is, in many ways, a story of characters. The start of the commercialisation of rating and reporting was dominated by Lewis Tappan, an imposing figure upon a number of disciplines. Yet, as we have just done, one can only understand Tappan by considering his whole story, what drove him and moulded him, and how he navigated his environment. To understand John Moody, we must do the same. The man who would create the company this book focuses upon has been chronicled in a small number of endeavours, but rarely in detail. In fact, the best source of information on the young Moody comes from his autobiography, *The Long Road Home*. The following analyses draw heavily on his work. However, there are corrections that need to be made.

Whilst Tappan was the great-grandnephew of Benjamin Franklin, John Moody's own ancestry is apparently more opulent still. John's ancestor, also named John Moody, was granted a knighthood and land in Bury St. Edmunds in the UK after saving the life of King Henry VIII. This is the story that John starts his autobiography with, of a young 'gentleman-in-waiting' called John Moody who saves King Henry VIII from drowning whilst crossing the River Thames in a small boat. According to John, his descendent was then rewarded with a knighthood and land. However, there is nothing to corroborate this story at all. In fact, the premise that King Henry nearly drowned in a small boat crossing the river is absolutely not true, and mistakes the reality that, whilst hunting:

> he was leaping a dyke with a hawking pole, when it suddenly broke, and the king was immersed in mud and water, and might have lost his life had not Edmund Moody, one of the falconers, immediately come to his assistance, and dragged him out.[56]

This story is corroborated by others,[57] and across a number of genealogy websites were budding genealogists have attempted to reveal the truth around the famous tale. It has been noted that Edmund Moody was rewarded with a Coat of Arms and not a knighthood, but did gain land in Bury St. Edmunds.

In his autobiography, John writes that his grandfather, another John Moody, 'decided to shake the dust of Seymour's Court from his feet and try his luck in the new world'. The Seymour's Court he refers to is an old monastery that had been converted into a palatial home, which John Moody suggests was given as a reward for his ancestor saving the King. In fact, the home was purchased by *a* Moody family via inherited wealth in 1776, but not John's family.[58] Whilst John's understanding seems to be wildly conflated with that of other genealogies – especially the family tree of what we may know today as the family that launched the Moody Bible Institute, founded by Dwight Lyman Moody, apparently the seventh-generation descendant of the Falconer who saved the King[59] – an analysis of a Moody bloodline that stems from Upton Lovel in Wiltshire, UK, reveals John's misunderstanding. The John Moody who our John Moody claims is his descendent arrived in the US in 1633 and died in 1655 in Hartford, Connecticut, but the first chronicled member of the Wiltshire bloodline (John Moody) died in 1658 in Wiltshire, three years later. Moody says that his grandfather:

> was born in 1793 at Beckington, Somersetshire, in a manor house which had originally been a monastery . . . for in the sixteenth century it had become

the home of Sir Thomas Seymour . . . this manor house then was, and still is, known as Seymour's Court

which aligns with the Wiltshire bloodline in that:

Thomas, fifth son of John, was born at Horningsham, in 1767, and moved to Seymour's Court, in 1776, with his parents. He succeeded his father as lease-holder of the estate, and, in 1792, married Anna Cross, of Maiden Bradley. They had nine children, all born at Seymour's Court: John, born 1793.[60]

John, born 1793, married Elizabeth Francis and had nine children, the youngest of which was William Francis, born 1834. John, in his autobiography, says that his grandfather moved from Seymour's Court and set sail for the US where, in Bridgeport, Connecticut, his father was born in 1834. In the Wiltshire bloodline, a William Francis is born in 1834. This is our John's Father. He married John's Mother, Miss Nichols, who the bloodline names as Jennie but who John names as Francis. Similarly, John suggests that his Mother was related to King Robert Bruce through her mother but, again, this cannot be corroborated.

John can be forgiven, writing in 1933, for his mistakes in his understanding. The ability to gather the necessary information was, of course, not as great as today. However, it does start to pull at the thread of the man who prides himself on his studiousness, his attention to detail, and his sense of self. The reality is that John did not know his lineage and conflated his knowledge of his lineage with that of a more romantic and noble understanding.

Nevertheless, and moving on, John describes how his grandfather was a 'dreamer, a poet, a rainbow chaser' who was not very good with money, always investing in things that would quickly go out of fashion or usefulness. Moody recounts that his grandfather 'was great cronies' with a man named Phineas T. Barnum, who some readers may recognise as the subject of the 2017 movie *The Greatest Showman*. Moody suggests that his grandfather turned down Barnum's offer to invest in his travelling circus and instead loaned him $500, which was never repaid (thus revealing his grandfather's poor business acumen). However, and again in questioning John's grasp of researched history, Barnum tells a different story in his autobiography, written in 1855 (which means John would have had an opportunity to consult this work himself before writing). Barnum tells how John Moody (our John's grandfather) allowed Barnum to purchase an interest in his grocery store at number 156 South Street in 1835. Barnum, who was in the process of setting up his travelling circus, was offered the opportunity to 'purchase a negress' – Joice Heth – who was apparently 161 years of age and a nurse to George Washington but who, in reality, was a blind and elderly Black woman, enslaved to the man selling her,[61] Mr Coley Bartram. Bartram offered Heth to Barnum for the price of $3000, but with the offer of a discounted rate of $1000 if certain conditions were met and in order to circumvent the law prohibiting slavery and the transferring of rights to people. Barnum arranged the sale of his piece of the grocery store back to Moody to finance the purchase.[62] In Moody's autobiography, it is perhaps telling that within the first four pages there are significant errors in his recounting of his familial history.

John was born in 1868. His mother gave birth to twelve children, but only five made it to maturity of which John was the oldest. He describes how his father's lack of business acumen resulted in the family experiencing cycles of fortune and despair in relation to the economy at the time, resulting in the young family moving from place to place throughout the New Jersey peninsula. A short stint in private school for John was curtailed when his father could no longer afford the fees, so John would spend his education in state schools. Raised in the Episcopal faith, John's family was very religious and instilled in the young man an adherence to the ways of the church. However, on a summer trip to his Uncle's farm in New England, the young John would have his faith tested for the first time whilst overhearing a conversation between his Uncle and a farmhand from Ireland. Faith, and its tenets, would become a central pillar in John's development, as the young man began to form a questioning approach to the environment around him.

In the autobiography, John tells quite amusing stories of his youth. He describes himself as a 'little scamp, [who] often got into trouble'. For example, he learned an early lesson after stealing his Uncle's prized horse and having it taken from him by members of a traveller's family, before his Aunt arranged for the horse to be returned. John suggests that his Uncle's revelations regarding the multiplicity of faith around the world misaligned his own value system. In what is quite a revealing anecdote about the young John's nature, he illustrates for us quite a joyous time in his life where he describes himself as a 'water-rat', a young boy amongst many who would frequent the lakes and rivers that were near to their homes. Self-described as the 'chief' of a boy's gang, John explains that he came up with an elaborate scheme to steal the attendance cards from his teacher whilst on detention and fraudulently submit them as cover for playing truant in a cave he and a friend had fitted out; this charade lasted from a November until the following April and he was only caught when, after stealing another horse from a farm, the horse led the young John straight to his own street! Tellingly, he says of his conscience, 'did my conscience trouble me? Not at all, as I remember. I reasoned – if I really did reason – that if the folks at home were to be deceived at all, it might as well be completely done'. After being disciplined by his father (with a switch), John proclaimed when asked if he would pray for forgiveness: 'I won't! I won't! There isn't any God, anyway! I heard Uncle John say so!'

After his mother's intervention, John relented and began to ask for forgiveness, first from God and then from his father. John's younger brother Willie was performing well academically and, because of John's truanting, he was put back two grades in school and fell far behind. In an effort to make the time up to escape the embarrassment of being out-performed by his sibling, John pleaded with the School principal to be put forward two grades if he promised to focus on his studies. The principal agreed and, borne out of desperation, the young John rapidly became excessively studious, catching up to his peers and in the mean-time developing a love for books, literature, and writing. He learned to compile information extensively, but also quickly, in a move that would stay with him throughout his career. Academically, John was striving. However, an economic crash destroyed any chance John had of attending college – with Princeton, Yale, and Columbia all being in his sights – and, instead, he was to enter the world of work at the age of 15.

After refusing to take communion on the grounds he could not, in good faith, receive it whilst questioning his faith, John would start work at a wholesale woodenware house in Washington Street, New York. He began writing for maga-zines after having an initial piece picked up by *The Boy's World*, which would transcend into dreams of starting his own journalistic career to which he would invest hundreds of dollars. To obtain that money he needed, after incurring debts with a publisher, John would push for a promotion which resulted in his ascen-sion to the till. Not content with the raise from two dollars to six dollars, Moody devised a scheme where he would lend money to other employees at a rate of 10% interest, and utilise his controlling of their wages as collateral. He borrowed the money from his younger sister's savings to initially finance this operation, and before long was fully 'now in the banking business!' Of course, it was more loan-sharking than banking, but Moody reasoned that 'it was better to have this rake-off come to me, to be used in my program of personal education and culture, than to let *all* of the money go to the grog shops' (a shop or room that sold alco-hol). The scheme lasted for a while, before one customer 'tuned state's evidence' and told the boss of the woodenware shop what was happening. He ordered John to stop immediately or lose his job, which John did. He had only saved enough to pay his debts to his publishers and his sister and so, at nineteen, he needed a new direction.

Moody began to study on correspondence courses offered by the Chautauqua Literary and Scientific Circle and went on to complete a number of courses, far in advance of those he would have been required to sit at college. This period further instilled in the young Moody the dedication to study that had allowed him to catch up to his peers when a younger boy. On this, he said:

> This intensive study period no doubt laid the groundwork for my plugging traits of later life. Boyhood days had taught me studious habits, but now I learned to guide and control my mind, to concentrate and reason logically.

At twenty-two, John had reached the end of his time at the shop. To bring in some money, he devised a plan to launch a regional newspaper to rival the two that dominated his small area around Bayonne. He started by including gossip about neighbours and stories about rivals and businesses. Before long, however, the young man who was not aware of the intricacies of libel law soon came to be educated, with a competitor threatening criminal libel charges 'with heavy damages'. Fearful, John's mother ordered him to stop the newspaper. During that time, Willie, John's younger brother, was making his way through a banking firm on Wall Street called Spencer Trask & Company, and after a word from his mother with her cousin, who was the senior banker George Foster Peabody at Spencer Trask, it was decided that John would follow his brother onto Wall Street.

John, with a modest but increased income, would quickly learn of the impact of economic cycles first hand. In his autobiography, he talks of an early encounter with a 'bucket shop', within which jobbers from around Wall Street would place illicit bets on the stocks their bosses were investing in, in the hope that they would continue to rise with the wave of the economy at the time. The young Moody recounts, however, that his new venture in gambling was ill-timed, as the Crash of 1893 wiped everybody out and cost Moody hundreds of dollars at the bucket shop. It seems, according to Moody, that the experience kept him away from the gambling scene on Wall Street and he instead focused on his work at Spencer Trask, especially under the mentorship of George, who he held in great regard.

It is difficult to pinpoint the reason for John's admiration of George, but it is a critical part of John's story. Speaking on this very matter, John states:

> we are all hero-worshipers in one way or another. My admiration for Peabody was not at all due to the fact that he happened to be a relative . . . perhaps more than all else, it was because, through the example of his forceful personality, I learned the importance and value of boldness and decision in business life.

Perhaps deeper than this, George represented a father-figure to be admired, especially as Moody consistently references the importance of stature and consequence, and to a greater extent perhaps, making one's mark on history. There is not much that John says about his father, except that during his early years at Spencer Trask John assumed the responsibility for the family and moved them to a quaint commuter village and away from the hustle and bustle that Bayonne had become; he notes, when recounting the move, that his father was unable to do this for the family on account of being in perpetual debt with local stores. Yet, John does detail one particular incident that left a mark on his early professional development, in which George rebuked John for not showing initiative and responding that he did not have the authority to complete a certain task by confirming for the impressionable John, 'Young man, you will never get anywhere in business if you wait for authority to come to you. All real men assume authority; only the dunces wait to have it conferred'.

This edict would stay with John forever. From that point on he took command of his own destiny, and soon came to outgrow Spencer Trask & Co., surmising that he would have to wait for too long to rise through the formal ranks, and even more so 'it was in my nature to want to steer my ship alone'. John wedded Anna M Addison in 1899,[63] and soon afterwards came to the realisation that he would need to venture into the world of business on his own. However, he was unsure as to how that would come about and, now into his thirties, he was anxious for the path forwards to be revealed to him. Whilst John was gaining a reputation for researching statistics, he says himself that 'despite a native distaste for mathematics, I had acquired the reputation of being the walking statistical table of the business'. It would therefore be happpenstance that would connect John to the world we now know he came to define, in that an article in the *Wall Street Journal* from editor Thomas F. Woodlock inspired Moody to ask a question of himself. Woodlock has argued in the piece that there was a need for greater knowledge and understanding of corporation statistics. Moody asked himself, 'somebody, sooner or later, will bring out an industrial statistical manual, and when it comes it will be a gold mine. Why not do it myself?' It is tempting, at least in a romanticised way, to suggest that 'this is where it all began' but, in doing so, we would ignore a lineage that provides insight into the trajectory of the credit rating industry that was about to ensue.

As an aside, it is worthwhile taking a moment to reflect on the development of some associated industries at this point in time. Whilst we will look formally in the next section at the start of Moody's as an entity, some stocktaking is important. Born in 1812 in Massachusetts,[64] Henry Varnum Poor had already begun to chart the path that John Moody would walk in the early 1900s. A lawyer by trade, Henry would enter the bourgeoning world of the American railroads in 1849 after his elder brother John purchased the American Railroad Journal, of which Henry would become Editor. He was the Editor from 1849 until 1862, after which he would launch what would become a seminal work in the *Manual of the Railroads of the United States*. Whilst Poor did not invent nor pioneer in the field of Manual development – Roger Babson details an interesting account of the Englishman Effingham Wilson who led the way in developing Manuals from 1805[65] – speaking on Poor's impact, Chandler notes that:

> As editor, compiler and analyst Henry Poor played a dual role in the highly dynamic business life of mid-nineteenth century America. In the first place, he pioneered in providing accurate and reliable business information and thus performed a new and essential function in a business world growing increasingly complex and specialised. The information he provided soon became invaluable to businessmen, promoters, entrepreneurs, and especially to investors. In a short time it came to be used by the government and much later by historians, economists and other students of American economic developments.[66]

What Henry built, technically, was something that was simply necessary for the time; without it, the expansion of the railroads would not have been possible.

Historians like Chandler rightly contextualise the Manual as more than an analytical document, and it seems that Poor agreed because, when writing to his wife, he proclaimed that:

> To tell you what I am doing would be to show you columns of figures to be added, divided, or subtracted, or the memoir of some railroad or canal, which is little else than a record of names and dates, and distances – all this is the most prosaic business possible. It may lay the foundation, by the by, for something better. First comes the form – then the soul, the natural sequence must be respected . . . I am getting along well though slowly. The work I am doing will never be done over again. So I am making it as valuable and complete as possible. It will be the record of a great achievement – of the greatest material development the world has yet seen.[67]

Before the Manual, the Journal had collated news and developments from across the varied railroad networks in one place, complete with annual reports from each railroad company and weekly share and bond lists. In a condensed tabular format, the Journal included statistical data 'for each listed road on mileage operated and mileage run, on equipment and other assets, on liabilities, earnings and dividends'. Critically, in 1852, Poor suspected that promoters coming to New York City to sell railroad mortgage bonds were potentially inflating their products and feared a boom, so, in turning his attention to what the investor may need instead of marketing for promoters, he changed the perspective of the Journal so that critical reports were written of each railroad. The report on the Erie Railroad in 1852 serves as a prime example of a notable change in emphasis from Poor, within which he strongly condemned the company for loading the company with debt and trying to hide this fact from investors. In a prophetic message perhaps, given the modern discussion around disclosure and transparency, Poor wrote:

> Other company tell is what they have done, and are doing, so why should not Erie? The public will demand the vouchers for the enormous sums that have gone into the road. They will be content no longer with general statement, which only mislead. Let us have details. Tell us, gentlemen, how many cubic yards of earth have been removed, how many feet of masonry and bridging have been constructed, how much rock has been excavated, and so on.[68]

The granularity of what Poor was analysing and conveying for the market was impressive. As an important aside, it is worth noting that even so early in the development of the industry, the market was responding positively and negatively to the authority of the raters. It is noted that there was a negative backlash from media and onlookers regarding the reach of Poor, but also positive changes made within the Erie Railroad company to affect what Poor had called for, in an effort to appease investors concerned by Poor's concerns. An unerring accuracy of prophesising railroad failures, based on his access to such granular data, only endeared him to investors more.

It is not hard to see then that something bespoke for the growing railroad arena was necessary. Poor believed that the best way to examine the potential future of an entity was to closely examine its history and, in that regard, he set about compiling the first ever chronicled history of the railroads and published the *History of the Railroads and Canals of the United States* in 1860, which was based on an approach of surveying every railroad company in the mid-1850s for specific information relating to their histories. This collation formed the backbone of what would become his *Manual of the Railroads of the United States*.[69] Henry would, in 1867 with his son, launch the H.V. and H.W. Poor Company, which would later become *Poor's Railroad Manual Company*.[70]

We were earlier introduced to the Bradstreet Company, who had pioneered the ranking of those they were building references on, and we have just been introduced to Henry Poor, who had pioneered the granular tabulation of statistics on the railroad industry, one of if not the driving force of the bourgeoning US economy. Friedman suggests that Moody benefitted directly from the work of Poor,[71] and I would second that; there is a lineage that Moody tapped into. It is interesting, therefore, that Moody neglects to make this connection in his autobiography and instead credits himself, based upon the reading of the *Wall Street Journal* article by Woodlock:

> Reading an article by Woodlock deprecating this paucity of needed information, one bright morning the thought flashed through my mind: 'Somebody, sooner or later, will bring out an industrial statistical manual, and when it comes it will be a gold mine. Why not do it myself?'. No doubt Mr Woodlock has long forgotten the incident, but a small, rather aggressive young man ventured into his office on Broad Street one day, outlined a plan for publishing a statistical manual, and asked him of his opinion on the scheme. 'A splendid idea', was his prompt reply. 'But it will take capital to put it on its feet. If you have financial backing, by all means go ahead'. That seemed to settle it; I would go ahead.

Much like the re-casting of his familial history, one suspects that John is re-casting the history of his formulating the idea for Moody's. The idea of a statistical manual had already been done very well by Poor and there is simply no way that John would not have known about it, given the wide utility of the Manual from Poor. Nevertheless, although Poor had moved into compiling information on more industries than just the railroad industry, he had stopped during some economic turbulence towards the end of the century, leaving a gap for somebody else to fill.[72]

John had one final hurdle in his way; a lack of capital. In what he calls a 'miracle', John describes how he was explaining his predicament to a colleague, a man named Eliphalet 'Liph' Potter, who offered his assistance in forming a partnership for the purposes of bringing John's idea to fruition. It turned out that $5000 was required to start, and Eliphalet raised it without much problem; he would stay on at Spencer Trask and go on to open his own investment banking firm, whilst John immediately left to focus on the Manual he was busy creating.

2.4 Credit Analysis for a New Era: The Birth of Moody's

It is worth repeating here that Moody did not invent 'credit ratings', but instead adapted an established genealogy that had existed for quite some time before him. Whilst the previous sections of this chapter illustrate this in detail, it is worth re-stating some truths:

> Ratings were to be an informational commodity whose value pertained to the measure of value. Although the service was new, the form of rating information was not. John Moody explicitly adopted an ordinal category format in 1909 as he began to publish his ratings of railroad bonds. This rating system had been previously developed and refined by mercantile agencies for the assessment of trade credit. It was already well known, a part of standard business practice for the management of credit, and so it provided an obvious and credible template. Many of the banks that purchased bonds already subscribed to the service of mercantile agencies, and so bank officials were familiar with the assessment of creditworthiness in terms of ordered categories. It was easy to translate that idiom from the evaluation of small businesses to bonds.[73]

Others attest to this lineage as we have already seen,[74] with Bostic and Orlando adding that Moody also utilised the foundation laid down by Poor and also the American Railroad Journal in the field of railroad statistics.[75] Sylla additionally, and helpfully, positions Moody's development within a wider developmental context:

> It was no accident of history, then, that Moody, the originator of the bond-rating agency, was an American, or that his original ratings were entirely for the bonded debts of U.S. railroads. The year was 1909, relatively late in the game given that the railroad bond market dated back to the 1850s, if not even earlier. It is evident that the corporate bond market, like the sovereign, bond market, could develop for a good long time without the benefit of independent agency ratings. How was that possible? And what led to the innovation of agency ratings?
>
> To answer those questions, we need to examine three historical developments, again largely American, that have to do with the ways in which lenders, creditors, and equity investors get information about borrowers, debtors, and equity shares that corporations issue. One is the credit-reporting (not

rating) agency. Another is the specialized financial press. A third is the investment banker. In a sense, the bond-rating agency innovated by Moody in 1909 represents a fusion of functions performed by these three institutions that preceded it.[76]

This amalgamation of utility would be propelled by the personal and professional development that John himself was undertaking. John was focused on the dynamics of the ever-growing dispersal of ownership being witnessed in the postbellum US; whilst only 12% of the US population owned shares by as late as 1929, its growth was relatively rapid and injected a new dynamic into the concept of investing, as John saw it.[77] John was keen to not only inject notions of science into the art of investing, but was also fascinated by the mindset of corporate titans and sought to reveal their workings, mannerisms, lives, and impact for the benefit of those willing to learn more, as exemplified by his writing of *The Masters of Capital* in 1920/21.[78] This is perhaps why historians have suggested that Moody's worldview was 'Dickensian in nature'. Nevertheless, he utilised this fascination in building a consistently developed portfolio of news and information on the corporate titans of the day, as well as a long list of other influential players, so that he could be ahead of the curve in terms of forecasting the marketplace. As Friedman suggests, Moody took this route rather than incorporating academic theory into his practice, something which Friedman confirms when he says that Moody was 'sceptical of professors, market theorists, and bureaucratic reformers'. It is against this backdrop that Moody first entered the rating field.

The publishing of John's *Moody's Manual of Industrial and Miscellaneous Securities*[79] is often cited as being the birthplace of the modern credit rating industry. However, before he had published the Manual, John created a detailed prospectus which he ferried around the lower echelons of New York City, before sending it further afield. He sent out five thousand copies of the prospectus along with blank order forms, including mailing the entire New York Stock Exchange Directory. His gamble, including using $200 of his own limited funds, proved to be worthwhile as he received several hundred orders for the book which he was yet to complete. Friedman notes how this promise of a 'humdinger' that would make Wall Street 'turn somersaults', together with the strong interest, meant that John had to utilise his skills of focusing and producing in a short period of time. With the assistance of his wife, Anna, John turned the Manual around and in 1900 fulfilled his orders and more. The Manual ran over 1100 pages and was bound in red to distinguish it from Henry Poor's volumes, which were bound in green.

The content was evolutionary, rather than revolutionary as we have already discussed. Yet, it was extremely well received. The book contained information on almost every railroad bond issued, alongside descriptive information about the railroad that issued them. It also contained 'an index [that] enabled any user to look up a particular bond with little trouble'.[80] For a number of reasons, the Manual hit the spot and was an instant success:

Moody then set about working tirelessly on the *Manual*, with the help of his wife, Anna. He completed it about seven or eight months later and it was published in 1900. Running to over 1,100 pages, the *Manual* had statistics on 1800 industrial companies and was bound in red to distinguish it from Poor's green-covered publications on railroads. Moody's manual had twelve sections, including ones on steel and iron, automobiles, mining, telephone and telegraph, and textiles. It listed company names, balance sheets, dates of incorporation, and outstanding securities (date of issue and value). The firms it covered had issued a total capital of $9.3 billion – a colossal amount of securities that, together with the railroads, were fuelling the growth of the nation. Though not nearly as well edited as Poor's manuals, it would improve over the years.

The first edition of the manual met with success of storybook proportions. Moody shrewdly had waited until after the distraction of the 1900 presidential election was over. When pro-business Republican William McKinley earned a second term and fought off the populist challenge of William Jennings Bryan, the stock market rallied – as did the market for investment advice. Moody's published 5,000 copies of the 1900 manual and sold them all at $5. His profits on the manual exceeded $500. Moody recalled in an autobiographical essay that he was so satisfied at the time that it seemed like 'rainbows were shining all around me'.[81]

John Moody's subsequent expansion was relatively rapid. He opened up a new office on Nassau Street and set up sales agencies for his Manual in Philadelphia, Chicago, Pittsburgh, London, and Amsterdam, with sales tours taking place in Cleveland, Chicago, Omaha, Denver, and California. By 1903, he had fifteen to twenty employees in his office. To cement this expansive phase, John launched the Moody Publishing Company in 1903 with a capital base of $125,000. The company embarked upon developing a financial library of over two thousand volumes of data on individual firms, and also a book publishing company specialising in the fields of finance and economics. Things were going so well, in fact, that John took Moody's public in 1904 with $1,000,000 in capital, in order to coordinate his many ventures, many of which were on a financed basis. His *Moody's Magazine* became a staple for business-minded people, but he went further and, perhaps in a nod to the gambling nature he demonstrated in his earlier years, took a punt on an expensive printing plant, a brick-making factory, and even a gold mine in Nevada.

It should not be surprising that, as things were going so well for John, others wanted to share the growing marketplace. Luther Blake, originally from

Tennessee, was in 1904 developing statistic 'cards' that would contain facts about leading companies, which promised more frequent updates than John's range of associated products. Yet, he did not invent this model of informational transmission, as Roger W Babson had launched his 'Babson Statistical Organisation' slightly earlier and developed the 'Babson Card System'. These cards were the first financial product produced by Babson after he exclusively turned his attention to business statistics, and they 'provided to subscribers descriptions on individual index cards of bonds offered by different companies. He soon started a parallel service with information about stocks'.[82] Blake incorporated Standard Statistics in 1906, and quickly developed a successful company that had hundreds of subscribers including the likes of J.P. Morgan & Co.; Blake would use bellboys from prominent hotels to deliver his cards around New York City. Yet, Blake and Babson had different products to Moody. Moody's direct competitor was Henry Poor, who had at that time incorporated Poor's Publishing Company. Poor, with his red-backed books, had developed two volumes on railroads and industrials that he sold for a combined $14; John sold his singular volume for $10.

This early phase of the rating industry, as it had developed from the reporting arena, enjoyed great successes in its earlier years. However, all that was to change in 1907. The Financial Panic of 1907, which transformed the face of American finance,[83] also had a transformative effect upon the bourgeoning credit rating industry. As for Moody himself, the effect was cataclysmic:

> With all of these businesses, Moody found himself overextended with the onset of the financial panic in 1907. The event arrived unexpectedly, Moody recalled, 'destroying values by the billions, replacing confidence with fear and foreboding, annihilating credit and driving up interest rates to the moon'. His 'house of cards collapsed with the rest, and all my business interests feel in ruin at my feet'. When the panic hit, Moody was thirty-nine years old and the father of two young boys, John and Earnest, aged seven and three. Faced with his failure and monumental debts, Moody contemplated suicide while staring out at the water off the Atlantic shore. Moody said of the period that he 'learned that uncontrolled optimism is no asset at all, but a great liability'.
>
> Moody's newspaper lost subscribers, the gold mine turned up nothing but mud, and the brick-making factory found little demand for its product during hard times. The printing plant, in particular, proved to be a burden, for it forced Moody to pay huge, fixed costs, in terms of plant operation, debt on the equipment, and payroll.[84]

Moody, somehow, managed to stave off personal bankruptcy. His professional endeavours however did not survive. The gold mine had revealed nothing, the printing press and brick factory went into receivership, and crucially so did his Manual Company. In February 1908, John was forced to sell his company to a group of creditors, including Eliphalet Potter. It would be Potter who would arrange for the company to be purchased by a long-term associate, but also a long-term rival of John – Roger Babson. So, in 1908, *Moody's Manual* was taken over by Babson, who immediately copyrighted the name Moody in association with industrial manuals, and prevented John from entering into the business for the foreseeable future. To grow the Manual, Roger added advertisements to the Manual, which allowed it to flourish during a time of great upheaval in the American financial sector. In a demonstration of the incestuous nature within the credit rating sector, Babson brought aboard a large number of analysts and information compilers from Poor's.

Interestingly, Babson, in his 1935 autobiography entitled *Actions and Reactions*, recounts his good-natured rivalry with John. He notes, with understandable pride, that:

> from that day to this, John Moody and I have been friendly but keen competitors. History must record that we revolutionised the collection, compilation, and publication of financial statistics. Although other concerns such as Standard Statistics . . . later came into the field and built up larger organisations, I doubt whether any outfit had had as good a time and has made as much money as John and I have.

He does however articulate something which the research in the earlier segments of the chapter revealed, when he says that 'unfortunately, John had a New York training instead of a New England training, and hence got caught in the panic of 1907'. In referring to the purchasing of the Manual Company, Roger finishes by saying that:

> Mr Potter, who was one of my clients, asked if I would be interested in purchasing the assets of the Moody Manual Company, which was to be sold at public auction. I replied that I had been a manufacturer of services and not a purchaser of services. I was benefiting from a lesson which I learned years previously – namely, that it is more profitable to manufacture bonds than to buy them! However, I was the only one who then had the necessary capital as well as the courage to supply it. I therefore took over the Moody Manual Company.[85]

Some in the literature make the mistake of viewing Moody's genealogy as being continuous. I suggest, and as I am illustrating throughout this book, that the control of an entity and the characters who demonstrate that control have too much of an influence to suggest that changes in ownership are inconsequential. For example, one scholar takes the ratings of *Moody's Manuals* between 1918 and 1939 as representative of the output of the company over that time period but,[86] as we shall see, there were a number of key developments once Moody had lost control which suggests greater care is needed. It is therefore worthwhile attempting to chart what happened, in the spirit of completing Moody's story.

After purchasing Moody's Manual Company in 1908, Babson hired his close colleague Roy Porter to be the editor of the Manual.[87] After losing control of his company, Moody briefly joined Luther Blake at Standard Statistics as the Editorial Supervisor of the Standard Bonds Description Service, but the collaboration was very short lived.[88] John Moody was prohibited from re-entering the statistic compilation business as part of his arrangement via the receivership, so instead John decided to monetise his forward-looking analyses that he was conducting for a time before via a number of business press outlets. He developed two products – *Moody's Weekly Letter* and *Monthly Analyses of Business Conditions* – which, just like his Manual, he peddled far and wide throughout New York. He quickly gained 100 subscribers and was recording profits in excess of $20,000 by 1911. Yet, all was not as it seemed as Moody, arguably illegally, utilised the subscription list that he had retained, against his agreement, from *Moody's Magazine* which had moved over to Babson in the sale; Roy Porter, speaking sometime later, denounced Moody's action as 'piracy'.

At the same time, Moody launched *Moody's Analyses Publishing*. It is this vehicle that would become the Moody's we know today. Friedman notes how more than fifty years after Bradstreet had pioneered the ranking (via letter [A-E]) of businesses, Moody's applied the very same sliding scale to corporates and their bond issuances; the first edition of Moody's *Analyses of Railroad Investments* contained the ratings of 1,200 bond issuances and hundreds of stocks. Obviously, this could be construed as being (dangerously for John) very close to the offering from *Moody's Manual*, so with that in mind John made the distinction in the introduction of his new work:

> For each firm, he included a description of the railroad line, as well as its location, mileage, equipment, income, expenses, and balance sheet. Moody was careful to distinguish this publication from his original manual. 'This is not a mere "manual" or statistical record of American railroads', he wrote in the introduction. 'It is much more than this. While it contains all the statistical records and other information required by the Banker, Broker, Financial Institution and Individual Investor . . . it also contains expert analysis of the railroad systems, showing the Physical Condition, Earning Power, Financial Characteristics and General Credit and standing of each of the companies'.[89]

Business boomed. Business boomed so much that after the panic of 1907 had subsided and the world was reorganising itself after the First World War, the financial arena for the credit rating entities was becoming much more changeable. In 1913, John Knowles Fitch launched the *Fitch Publishing Company* and, back at the Moody's Manual Company, Babson was busy selling his positions in his many endeavours, including his control of Moody's Manual Company, to Roy Porter (though Babson remained a shareholder). Interestingly, Moody recounts how Babson tried to warn John of a coming downturn – Roger was a keen follower of cyclical-based theories of market development – although John wrote this off as 'a Babson trick'. As part of Babson's retreating, Luther Blake purchased the Babson bond card system in 1913 and incorporated *Standard Statistics* a year later in 1914. That same year, John formed *Moody's Investors Service* as an umbrella corporation to control the ratings and weekly letter businesses, with the founding motto being 'founded to endure and investors make secure'. In 1916 the Poor's Manual Company would formally enter the rating arena, but in 1919 Roy Porter would purchase the company and merge it with the original Moody's Manual Company – which would operate under Poor's name. As you can see, there is a lot of industrial reorganisation occurring in the early years of the rating industry, and more was to come.

For Moody, however, he was to capitalise on his successes. The intra-war years were difficult for a number of reasons, but Moody stood out for his seemingly tight grasp on the world of business and its development. Early and bullish analyses of particular sectors and how they would respond to the First World War, which would prove to be accurate, led to Moody being labelled as 'almost an oracle in the financial world'.[90] Moody was self-congratulatory when his predictions on the development of the market as the years moved into the 1920s led to a sharp increase in sales and profits; for example, the company's profits ballooned to $271,000 in 1928, based upon revenues of $1.8 million. It was also noted that Moody, his ratings, and his predictions, were becoming 'standard tools for assessing risks amongst investors'.[91]

The 1920s were going so well for John that, in 1924, he bought back his own name.[92] This was not insignificant for John, who resented his losing control of the original company – then under control by Roy Porter after Babson's retreat – and Friedman notes how:

> by 1924, Moody paid $100,000 to repurchase the rights to the name *Moody's Manual* from Roger Babson and his associate Roy Porter. He thought this was a very good deal. He wrote in a memoir that he was ready to pay $250,000 had they asked.[93]

Further to this reunification, Moody expanded by opening regional offices in Chicago and Los Angeles in 1925, and then London a short while later.

Interestingly, and perhaps underscoring the modus operandi of the company right up until the aftermath of the Financial Crisis (which we will cover in a later chapter), Moody never once revealed his methodologies. Friedman notes how:

> From his days working at Spencer Trask forward, Moody had acquired a tremendous bird's-eye view of business. He, like many of the clients he served, was entirely future-oriented in his business ambitions – always adding to his

services, reorganising his company, adding new branches, and securing new audiences. His forecasts reflected this sense of mastery over the details of individuals and also a sense of which industries offered opportunities.

However, in relation to the methodological underpinnings of his predictions:

> Moody never published an article describing his method of forecasting. He rejected simple or mechanical ways of judging the trend of business activity, distrusting the notion that business trends moved in a uniform or reliable sequence. Moody did not theorise on the nature of the business cycle. When pushed, he gave an explanation of the business cycle in psychological terms, not unlike Babson: 'business must alternate from good to bad and back again, because it can do nothing else. A cycle is merely this inevitable alternation. Most business changes are due to universal human traits and instincts, or, in other words, to psychology as expressed in mercantile affairs. Successes tend to make even the greatest of men over-confident, while failures make us all humble'. But he did not believe, like Babson, that there was an exact equivalence between ups and downs. He did not think that business cycles were alike; he believed that there were many variations in their underlying causes and consequences.[94]

This belief was to become critically important. In 1928 Moody moved offices whilst riding a wave of optimism: from Nassau Street to 65 Broadway. Moody's move may have been impacted by Blake's decision to take up a fancy new office space in nearby Varick Street, but irrespective of this there was a hubris enveloping Wall Street at the time. Moody's ratings books were selling well and his position as an 'oracle' was steadily being cemented. On the back of this hubris, and in what was a pivotal move for him personally and professionally, John took Moody's public. Critically, 'Moody bought out the shares of several other investors. All this loaded Moody with 32,000 of 60,0000 shares of common stock just prior to the 1929 crash'.

We will not cover the Crash of 1929 here in any great detail, as others have so wonderfully done,[95] but the important consideration for us was that John Moody was entirely caught out by it. On October 28, 1929 – one of the worst days of the crash – Moody wrote in his *Weekly Letter* that:

> we are convinced that it represents nothing more or less than a speculator's frenzy of fear for the time being – in other words, a technical condition of the market rather than a reflection of radically changing underlying conditions, which, in point of fact, remain relatively stable.

Friedman notes the contrast between Moody and the already-retreated Babson: 'with those words, Moody joined the other forecasters who failed to anticipate the stock market crash. Moody was embarrassed that his nemesis, Roger Babson, had gained popular recognition for predicting it. Moody found it difficult to comprehend what had happened'.[96] One of the major issues for Moody was that his methodologies, for want of a better word, were based upon his understanding of business' projections. Clearly, very few companies would have projected the Crash and ensuing depression that would become the Great Depression, and herein lay Moody's weakness. For those who studied historical markers of downturns and upturns, the ability to see the Depression coming was easier.

That failure had a direct consequence for Moody and Moody's. In 1929 Moody's recorded revenues of more than $3.5 million, but in 1931 those revenues had plummeted to $500,000. They did increase momentarily to $2 million in 1932 but would not reach the $3.5 million mark and beyond for another *twenty-five* years. A period of significant cost-cutting was underway at Moody's, and in the early 1930s, he ceased producing the *Weekly Letter*. Perhaps in a representative move that confirms the effect of the time upon John's thinking, he moved away from forecasting altogether and instead started to really focus on the realities of securities and their 'worthiness', as well as increasing the private consulting the firm undertook. Though not immediately lucrative, the change in focus would be a prophetic one.

The 1930s marked a sharp about-turn in American economic, legal, and political thinking. Unsurprisingly, given the seismic nature of the Crash and the ensuing Depression, the needs of those tasked with running the system, and those within and exposed to the system, fundamentally changed. Yet, the ratings that made up the core of the rating industry were entirely untested and, as we saw with Moody's refusal to shed light on his methodological processes, it was unknown how the agencies arrived at their destinations with each rating. Carruthers says, of the ratings, that 'their ubiquity in the marketplace was taken as prima facie evidence of their value'[97] which is fine when it is investors and issuers who freely decide to utilise the ratings. The sentiment here is that it is up to the market to decide whether they are useful given they could not see behind the veil. Flandreau and his colleagues, over the span of several fantastic articles, detail how the outputs of the mercantile agencies and then the rating agencies were woven into judicial decisions, thus either recognising, validating, or perhaps both the status of the agencies and their outputs. In 1931, as a response to a wave of defaults and plummeting bond prices, the Office of the Comptroller of the Currency 'instituted formulae based on credit ratings to book the value of US national banks' bond portfolios'.[98] Then, in early 1936, the Comptroller promulgated a rule that formally forbade national banks from investing into securities marked as 'speculative'; to demarcate between the strength of securities, the Comptroller used the demarcation developed by the rating agencies between 'investment-grade' and as we would know it today, 'non-investment grade' or 'speculative'. This was quickly followed by the Investment Company Act of 1940 that precluded particular funds from investing in similarly speculative securities.

There are several reasons why the Comptroller took these actions in the 1930s. One is that the banks were coming under considerable public pressure for their role in the origination of the products that had brought the country to its knees; the rating agencies, on the other hand, merely sold Manuals that attempted to understand the market – they had no role, then, in the origination of securities. That distance provided the Comptroller, and the agencies, with the necessary independence to be inducted into the framework as a method in which the model of operation within the banking sector could be curtailed and controlled. Interestingly, the initial approach was that any rating would do from any of the 'statistical rating organisations', but this was soon buttressed with the provision that, in 1936 via the Comptroller's announcement to the national banks, 'such eligibility must be supported by not less than two rating manuals'.[99]

Perhaps unsurprisingly, or not, this move to effectively outsource risk assessment on a national basis drew heavy criticism from those within the financial system and had immediate effects. The move meant that, almost overnight, half of the bonds traded on the New York Stock Exchange could no longer be purchased by affected institutions, with a notable banker's association quoted as saying that the 'delegation of the judgment as to what constitutes a sound investment is unprecedented in our history and wholly unwarranted by [the agencies] records in the past'. Even though the Comptroller succumb to the pressure and injected some level of flexibility into the operations of the national banks, the dye was cast.

For Moody himself, his business journey was almost at an end. Managing to keep Moody's afloat during the Crash and the Depression took its toll. The intervention of the regulatory framework had helped Moody's, though their competitors were struggling. Poor's Manual Company, which had suffered losses on the back on publication investments, first sold its subscription list to Moody's in 1940 in an attempt to survive, and then when that failed was bought out by Standard Statistics, resulting in the ignominy of forever having its name come second in the tie-up.[100] John had started to spend more time concerned with religious pursuits and, in 1944 he retired as the President of Moody's Investment Services. His intense focus on Catholicism and the Church resulted in his being made a Knight Commander of the Order of the Holy Sepulchre of Jerusalem, the second in a rank of five prestigious awards within the Catholic faith. John moved to La Jolla near San Diego in 1957 and passed away just a year later.

2.5 Conclusion

The story of credit rating agencies is, in a lot of ways, a story of strong characters. That is the case in the modern day, to an extent, but it is certainly the case when we look at the origins of the industry. Of course, the stories of each of the men we have profiled are very different, but in a number of ways they are remarkably similar. Theirs is a story of tremendous intelligence, but one also of luck, happenstance, opportunity, greed, and very interestingly when they came to reflect, regret. Whether that is instructive to us as we attempt to take a wide lens to the concept of credit rating, utilising Moody's as a focal point, I perhaps leave to you as the reader.

Credit ratings are, essentially, judgements. They are judgements apparently made by impartial entities, and with the support of masses of relevant data, but in the end, they are merely judgements. This raises an associated question: who are they to judge? The earliest machinations of the concept were trade bodies and then established multinational banking and trade houses, which perhaps gives an answer to our question; their capital was at risk. Their *need* to judge was acute. However, the commercialisation of the concept perhaps brings forth a very different answer. Lewis Tappan's successful commercialisation of the judging process was led by a man who disavowed racism and slavery on one hand and actively worked with outwardly racist and pro-slavery people and regions on the other. John Moody, who apparently stood for transparency and honesty in the marketplace, had a track record of lying, gambling, and who judged countless entities without ever revealing the method with which he did so. The installing of a third-party in the creditor and debtor relationship fundamentally removes the accountability and, arguably, the authority to judge. Nevertheless, we now have a multi-billion dollar industry today.

The fact that despite the criticism levelled at the mercantile agencies for infiltrating social fibres (by way of encouraging spying and tale-telling), and the criticism levelled at the early rating agencies for being undeserving of the regulatory authority given to them, the reality is that the men we profiled provided, in differing forms and often on the practical and ideological backs of others, crucial services. There is, unsurprisingly, debate as to how crucial those services are in reality, but I have argued elsewhere that it is the *signal* that a rating allows one party to send to another, or others, that is its true utility. Perhaps what we have learned in this chapter supports that, as despite mercantile agencies producing reports that quickly became outdated, or rating agencies producing ratings and forecasts that had no understood methodological basis and missed massive financial catastrophes, their growth continued. It would take quite a while for Moody's to return to the heights of the 1920s, but it would, and it would do so in an unprecedented manner.

John Moody, in the final pages of *The Long Road Home*, reflects on his life and his conversion to Catholicism. It is telling that, throughout his autobiography, the Father of modern credit ratings rarely addresses his business successes and instead decides to prioritise the telling of his spiritual development. A page from the end, he says the following which is very instructive indeed:

It *is* disconcerting to see a supposedly sane businessman, whose life has been spent in the marts of trade, suddenly make a handspring out of this gloriously enlightened twentieth century, and land in the dim religious light of the thirteenth. Surely there must be a screw loose somewhere.

But perhaps some of those who have read this story, though they may not see the supernatural way of grace, may get a glimmer of the meaning just the same. They may notice, for instance, that I had for some time harboured a strange notion that political, social, and economic problems are, at bottom, moral problems . . . we are being told nowadays that what we used to call the moral law is archaic and obsolete. The golden rule is that there is no golden rule, says Bernard Shaw. Morals have become mere conventions, folkways; always to be revamped to suit the passing spirit of the times. And out of this enlightened view we have before our eyes a wrecked and ruined world, crippled by greed and selfishness.

. . . that I was long a victim to this modern temper, he who runs may read.[101]

Was John a victim? A victim of his time, or perhaps of his environment? Or was John a cause of the modern temper he attributes to developing a 'modern world headlong to hell'? It is perhaps up to you, as the reader, to decide the answers to those questions. Yet, Babson's suggestion that John lost everything in the Panic of 1907 because of his New York-upbringing and training, as opposed to Roger's New England beginnings, arguably provides us with some insight into the makings of John Moody. A man clearly in possession of an incredible intellect, his surroundings failed him. Despite that, and many attempts to veer off-course, his innate abilities managed to carry him through and, I would strongly argue, into infamy. His name is now synonymous with an entire industry, and his name which he so tirelessly chased to recover, now is in the headlines almost every day. John represents a man who was willing to inflate his story but who also focused on the fine minutiae of thousands of others' stories; what he represents is, in many ways, complex. As we shall see in the remaining chapters, the institution he built is also defined by its complexity.

Notes

1 John Moody, *A Long Road Home* (Palgrave Macmillan 1933) vii.
2 Walter Friedman, *Fortune Tellers: The Story of America's First Economic Forecasters* (Princeton UP 2013) 89.
3 Robert J Bennett, 'Supporting Trust: Credit Assessment and Debt Recovery Through Trade Protection Societies in Britain and Ireland, 1776–1992' (2012) 38 Journal of Historical Geography 123–42, 126.
4 For more on Trade Protection Societies see: David Philips, *Crime and Authority in Victorian England: The Black Country, 1835–1860* (Croom Helm 1977).
5 Ralph W Hidy, 'Credit Rating Before Dun and Bradstreet' (1939) 13(6) Bulletin of the Business Historical Society 81.
6 Flandreau and Mesevage discuss how de Rothschild was accused of seeking to 'purchase a US President to taste' after the Civil War, see: Marc Flandreau and Gabriel G Mesevage, 'The Separation of Information and Lending and the Rise of the Rating Agencies in the USA (1841–1907)' (2014) 62 Scandinavian History Review 3.

7 For a short and sharp account of the role that Baring Brothers played in the Louisiana Purchase, see Junius P Rodriguez, *The Louisiana Purchase: A Historical and Geographical Encyclopaedia* (ABC-CLIO 2002) 25.
8 Jessica M Lepler, *The Many Panics of 1837: People, Politics, and the Creation of a Transatlantic Financial Crisis* (CUP 2013).
9 Hidy (n 5) 85.
10 Rowena Olegario, *A Culture of Credit: Embedding Trust and Transparency in American Business* (Harvard UP 2006) Chapter 2.
11 James H Madison, 'The Evolution of Commercial Credit Reporting Agencies in Nineteenth-Century America' (1974) 48(2) The Business History Review 164–86, 166.
12 Olegario (n 10) 229.
13 Edward J Balleisen, 'Vulture Capitalism in Antebellum America: The 1841 Federal Bankruptcy Act and the Exploitation of Financial Distress' (1996) 70(4) The Business History Review 473–516, 495.
14 ibid.
15 ibid.
16 Phyllis M Bannan, *Arthur and Lewis Tappan: A Study of Religious and Reform Movements in New York City* (Columbia Dissertations Publishing 1950) 4.
17 Scott A Sandage, *Born Losers: A History of Failure in America* (Harvard UP 2006) 105.
18 National Abolition Hall of Fame and Museum, 'Lewis Tappan' (2022) <www.national abolitionhalloffameandmuseum.org/lewis-tappan.html>.
19 Bannan (n 16) 6.
20 Barry Hankins, *The Second Great Awakening and the Transcendentalists* (Greenwood Press 2004) 97.
21 Bannan (n 16) 9.
22 Olegario (n 10) 46.
23 Dana L Robert, *Occupy Until I Come: AT Pierson and the Evangelisation of the World* (Wm B Eerdmans Publishing Company 2003) 3.
24 James B Stewart, *Abolitionist Politics and the Coming of the Civil War* (Massachusetts UP 2008) 78.
25 Claudine L Ferrell, *The Abolitionist Movement* (Greenwood Press 2006) 131. For more on the *La Amistad* case and Tappan's involvement see: Iyunolu F Osagie, *The Amistad Revolt: Memory, Slavery, and the Politics of Identity in the United States and Sierra Leone* (Georgia UP 2000); David Hulm, *United States v The Amistad: The Question of Slavery in a Free Country* (The Rosen Publishing Company 2004); Bernell E Tripp, 'Lewis Tappan and the Friends of Amistad: The Crusade to Save the Abolition Movement' in David B Sachsman, SK Rushing and Roy Morris (eds), *Words at War: The Civil War and American Journalism* (Purdue UP 2008); Marcus Rediker, *The Amistad Rebellion: An Atlantic Odyssey of Slavery and Freedom* (Verso 2013).
26 Bertram Wyatt-Brown, 'God and Dun & Bradstreet, 1841–1851' (1966) 40(4) The Business History Review 432–50, 437.
27 Olegario (n 10) 41.
28 ibid.
29 Sandage (n 17) 109.
30 Olegario (n 10) 40.
31 Marc Flandreau and Gabriel G Mesevage, 'The Untold History of Transparency: Mercantile Agencies, the Law, and the Lawyers (1851–1916)' [2014] Enterprise and Society 220.
32 Sandage (n 17) 101.
33 Olegario (n 10) 45.

34 Madison (n 11) 174.
35 Sandage (n 17) 156.
36 Wyatt-Brown (n 26) 442.
37 Sandage (n 17) 111.
38 Wyatt-Brown (n 26) 110.
39 Madison (n 11) 169.
40 Wyatt-Brown (n 26) 440.
41 Madison (n 11) 172.
42 Chester Arthur Phillips, *Bank Credit: A Study of the Principles and Factors Underlying Advances Made by Banks to Borrowers* (Palgrave Macmillan 1931) 215.
43 Madison (n 11) 165.
44 Edward Neville Vose, *Seventy-Five Years of The Mercantile Agency RG Dun & Co 1841–1916* (RG Dun & Co 1916).
45 Madison (n 11) 172. The seminal case that developed this doctrine was *Eaton v Avery* (1880) 83 NY 34.
46 For examples of such malpractice see: Sandage (n 17); Flandreau and Mesevage (n 31) 221; Madison (n 11) at various points of their work.
47 Flandreau and Mesevage (n 31) 229.
48 Sandage (n 17) 184.
49 Madison (n 11) 181.
50 Flandreau and Mesevage (n 31) 223.
51 Sandage (n 17) 148.
52 Madison (n 11) 177.
53 Richard Sylla, 'An Historical Primer on the Business of Credit Rating' in Richard M Levich, Giovanni Majnoni and Carmen Reinhart (eds), *Ratings, Rating Agencies and the Global Financial System* (Springer 2002) 23. Dun initially fought the concept of standardised ratings (within the new Bradstreet book) but competition forced his hand and RG Dun & Co adopted the product: see Howard Bodernhorn, 'Credit Rating Agencies' in Charles R Geisst (ed), *Encyclopaedia of American Business History* (Facts on File 2006) 110.
54 Martha Poon, 'Rating Agencies' in Karin K Cetina and Alex Preda (eds), *The Oxford Handbook of the Sociology of Finance* (OUP 2012) 276.
55 Bruce G Carruthers, 'Credit Ratings and Global Economic Governance: Non-Price Valuation in Financial Markets' in Gregoire Mallard and Jerome Sgard (eds), *Contractual Knowledge: One Hundred Years of Legal Experimentation in Global Markets* (CUP 2016) 327.
56 Royal Institution of Great Britain, *Notices of the Proceedings at the Meetings of the Members of the Royal Institution of Great Britain*, vol XIII (William Clowes and Sons Ltd 1893) 359.
57 BJ Bradley, *Henry VIII: Man or Myth* (Lulu 2005) 37.
58 Sarah Moody Alvord, *Genealogy of the Moody Family* (Unknown 1916) 10.
59 Rick Lindholtz, *Pleasant Lines* (Lulu 2014) 19.
60 Alvord (n 58) 11.
61 Barnum has since been chronicled and studied in full, see: Benjamin Reiss, *The Showman and the Slave: Race, Death, and Memory in Barnum's America* (Harvard UP 2010).
62 Phineas T Barnum, *The Life of PT Barnum* (Sampson Law, Son & Co 1855) 150.
63 Friedman (n 2) 91.
64 Alfred D Chandler, *Henry Varnum Poor: Business Editor, Analyst, and Reformer* (Arno Press 1981).

65 Roger W Babson, *Actions and Reactions: An Autobiography of Roger W Babson* (Harper & Brothers 1935) 103.
66 Alfred D Chandler, 'Henry Varnum Poor: Business Analyst' (1950) 2(4) Explorations in Entrepreneurial History 180.
67 ibid 187.
68 ibid 183.
69 Rawi Abdelal, *Capital Rules: The Construction of Global Finance* (Harvard UP 2007) 167.
70 Richard S Wilson and Frank J Fabozzi, *Corporate Bonds: Structures & Analysis* (Frank J Fabozzi Associates 1996) 211.
71 Friedman (n 2) 92.
72 ibid.
73 Carruthers (n 55) 327.
74 Jerome Fons, 'White Paper on Rating Competition and Structured Finance' (2008) <https://oversight.house.gov/sites/democrats.oversight.house.gov/files/documents/Fons%20Ratings%20White%20Paper.pdf>.
75 Raphael W Bostic and Anthony W Orlando, 'When the Invisible Hand isn't a Firm Hand: Disciplining Markets That Won't Discipline Themselves' in Lee A Fennell and Benjamin J Keys (eds), *Evidence and Innovation in Housing Law and Policy* (CUP 2017) 325.
76 Richard Sylla, 'A Historical Primer on the Business of Credit Ratings' (Prepared for the Conference, The Role of Credit Reporting Systems in the International Economy for the World Bank, Washington, 1–2 March 2001) 6.
77 Friedman (n 2) 86.
78 John Moody, *The Masters of Capital: A Chronicle of Wall Street* (Yale UP 1920).
79 John Moody, *Moody's Manual of Industrial and Miscellaneous Securities* (OC Lewis Co 1900).
80 Carruthers (n 55) 327.
81 Friedman (n 2) 93.
82 ibid 18.
83 For a very readable account of the effect of the 1907 Panic, see: Robert F Bruner and Sean D Carr, *The Panic of 1907: Heralding a New Era of Finance, Capitalism and Democracy* (John Wiley & Sons 2023).
84 Friedman (n 2) 98.
85 Babson (n 65).
86 Norbert Gaillard, *A Century of Sovereign Ratings* (Springer 2011) 40.
87 Richard C Wilson and Frank J Fabozzi, *Corporate Bonds: Structure and Analysis* (John Wiley & Sons 1995) 210.
88 ibid 211.
89 Friedman (n 2) 101.
90 ibid 107.
91 ibid 108.
92 Wilson and Fabozzi (n 87) 210.
93 Friedman (n 2) 108.
94 ibid 110.
95 Perhaps one of the more famous and representative examples is: James K Galbraith, *The Great Crash, 1929* (Houghton Mifflin Harcourt 1997).
96 Friedman (n 2) 114.
97 Bruce G Carruthers, 'From Uncertainty Toward Risk: The Case of Credit Ratings' (2013) 11 Socio-Economic Review 525–51, 537.

98 Marc Flandreau, Norbert Gaillard and Frank Packer, 'Rating Performance, Regulation and the Great Depression: Lessons from Foreign Government Securities' (2009) Working Paper in International History and Politics, 3 <https://repository.graduateinstitute.ch/record/4088/files/WP-2011-019.pdf>.
99 ibid 9.
100 Raymond A Anderson, *Credit Intelligence and Modelling* (OUP 2022) 275.
101 Moody (n 1) 258.

3 From Here to Eternity

3.1 Introduction

After John had retired in 1944, the company settled into its newly-found oligopolistic position alongside the newly-formed S&P, and latterly Fitch. There are not many accounts of this particular time period up until the late 1960s, with even the Moody's website only starting their review of their own history in 1970. What is perhaps clear is that the so-called 'Quiet Period' after the Second World War was not a lucrative one for Moody's, as it found itself caught between a major event in human history and before the real start of technological innovation that would transform the financial sector irrevocably. Yet, the 1960s and 1970s would prove to be pivotal turning points in the history of Moody's and in this chapter, we shall see how, but more importantly why.

We shall see how the credit rating agencies' influence was waning and, threatened with technological developments that threatened their fundamental ability to receive compensation for their efforts, the rating agencies were left to the mercy of fate. Quite opposed to popular theories of rating agencies changing their models to take advantage of market conditions, we shall see a counternarrative that continues our approach of joining together *all* of the dots between the many facets of the sprawling and intertwined credit rating and reporting industries. The rate of change in the fortune of the credit rating agencies was remarkable and I am reminded of the 1953 American war film starring Burt Lancaster, Montgomery Clift, Deborah Kerr, and a young Frank Sinatra named *From Here to Eternity*, as an illustrative title for this turnaround given that, since this period, the rating agencies have not looked back.

It is also the case that this time period provides us with yet more insight into the *culture* and *nature* of credit rating agencies, and in that I fully include Moody's as perhaps the epitome. There have been several analyses that paint the rating agencies as benign benefactors of situational developments, but we shall see that this understanding could not be further from the truth. We shall see an engrained culture of preservation of self, combined with the ability to cause great harm and come out the other side unscathed. That dynamic is repeated throughout the

DOI: 10.4324/9781003001065-3

history of Moody's, but the 1970s provides us with a sharply focused picture of that dynamic in action. We will also see how popular narratives, whether by design or by accident, distort this identification of an underlying culture by either misrepresenting the true order of development within the industry or by ignoring key junctures altogether. To get a full story of something, one needs to address each and every development.

3.2 Correcting the Record: The Penn Central Picture

As discussed above, the time between John Moody retiring and the company heading into the 1970s was seemingly a quiet one. Outside of official histories produced for internal use only at Moody's, there is not much to be found on developments within the company during this time period. However, all fingers point to the marketplace being unkind to Moody's and other rating agencies, given that in 1962 Moody's was bought out by Dun and Bradstreet, who had merged in 1933 (more on this shortly); consequently, S&P was bought out by McGraw-Hill just four years after Moody's was integrated into Dun and Bradstreet. Whilst accurate records of the time period are hard to come by, there have been theories and suggestions as to why:

As quickly as credit rating agencies were able to accumulate reputational capital during their meteoric rise of the early 1930s, they just as quickly squandered such capital during the following years. As a result, credit rating agencies did not remain important or influential for long. Following their heyday in the 1920s and 1930s, the agencies experiences austerity and contraction during the 1940s and 1950s. during this period, bond prices were not volatile, the economy was healthy, and few corporations defaulted. As a consequence, both the demand for and the supply of relevant credit information dwindled. The rating agencies were struggling when John Moody died in 1958. According to the reputational capital view, the decline of the rating agencies would have been a response to their inability to generate accurate and valuable information after the early 1930s.[1]

Whilst I am not a follower of the reputational capital theory, for several reasons, it is true to say that the agencies were undergoing a period of contraction in the 1940s, 1950s, and 1960s. However, not everybody was suffering. To understand why the *credit rating agencies* were suffering, one needs to step back and withdraw the focus on the picture. What follows is a correction of the record to show just why the rating agencies were suffering, and how they turned it around.

Unfortunately, it will be difficult to remain in a linear pattern in our story. To go back in the story means, at times, to go forward. For example, to provide you with the necessary context, in 1970 one of the largest railroad companies in the US – Penn Central – defaulted on all of its commercial paper, which are relatively short-term lending vehicles. The following is, perhaps, representative of the accepted and popular understanding of its importance to the development of rating agencies:

> During the Vietnam War, bond price volatility increased somewhat, as did issuance of commercial paper, and borrowers faced a severe credit contraction. Demand for credit information increased during this period, but the agencies remained relatively small and not obviously important as a source of information to issuers or investors. At the time, the rating agencies employed only a few analysts each and generated revenues primarily from the sale of published research reports. The market did not place great value on those research reports, presumably, according to the reputational capital view, because rating agencies had lost a large portion of their reputational capital. Moreover, as the commercial paper market expanded rapidly during the 1960s, investors were not very precise in assessing credit quality. In the fallout of the 1970 Penn Central default on $82 million of commercial paper, investors began demanding more sophisticated levels of research. The rating agencies, still relatively small and without substantial reputational capital, were not in a position to satisfy this demand.[2]

Partnoy then goes on to suggest, in a number of works, that it was the SEC's decision to promote the concept of a 'Nationally Recognised Statistical Rating Organisation' in 1973 that gave the rating agencies the position to satisfy such demand, and that the rest was history. This is, essentially, the 'reputational capital' view, in that it proposes that regulators have inserted the rating agencies into the financial sector in a manufactured manner, and that this provides them with all the protection they need. It is a popular view, but it has been challenged. The works of Marc Flandreau and his colleagues over a number of works present an opposing theory, namely the 'legal licence' view that shows the rating agencies merely being recognised by the courts, and then the regulators, as part of a market-accepted suite of mechanical assistance options that it uses, and then codified as such: one view paints the regulators as instigators of market practice, the other paints regulators as followers of market practice.

Nevertheless, you can see how we had to jump forward in our story. But, by reducing the lens with which we are examining Moody's, a different and more accurate truth is revealed. The collapse of Penn Central, which according to the popular view happened because the trading of commercial paper – a growing and prevalent option for financing at the time – happened without the support of any third-party verification or guidance, is a crucial part of the story. As Hudson claims:

> The use of credit ratings is a prerequisite in almost all Commercial Paper (CP) markets. The real use of ratings began in the USCP market following the

failure in 1970 of Penn Central with $82 million of CP outstanding. At that time, investors relied on name recognition as the principal criterion for issuer selection. Now, even though buyers of CP must make their own credit assessment, much reliance is placed on the independent commercial rating agencies to establish the creditworthiness of borrowers. Although the SCP market started without the need for borrowers to be rated, this is not the case now.[3]

This understanding is only correct if you view the credit rating agencies, and the concept of third-party support, in a silo which, by this point in the book, we know should never be the case. In going back further still to help us understand developments, some more industrial reorganisation needs to be discussed.

In getting closer to his retirement, Lewis Tappan handed over the reins of the Mercantile Agency to Benjamin Douglass, who would expand the Mercantile Agency's reach exponentially. As time passed, Benjamin passed the control of the agency to his brother-in-law, Robert G. Dun, who would go on to rename the agency in his own name – R.G. Dun & Co. At the same time, John Bradstreet's own credit reporting agency was solidly positioning itself as Dun's main competitor, providing the market with a number of innovations which John Moody himself adapted for the young Moody's companies. This we know already. Yet, Dun brought in a man named Arthur D. Whiteside in 1931 who would both quickly become the agency's CEO, and also bring with him his own endeavour, the *National Credit Office* (NCO).[4] In 1933, Whiteside pulled off perhaps one of the largest and most famous mergers of the time, bringing together the historic companies of Dun and Bradstreet, to form Dun & Bradstreet.[5] According to D&B's own website, 'whereas previously both companies sold "products", Whiteside increasingly emphasised "service". With great leadership, he led D&B out of the Depression and into the Information Age'.[6]

Whiteside passed away in 1960, after changing the culture of the reporting industry to a culture of 'service', which is substantially different in concept to selling products. Whiteside would become an adviser to Presidents, perhaps becoming the living embodiment of this change in culture. Yet, in the 1960s Whiteside's successor, J. Wilson Newman, embarked upon extending D&B's footprint and range of services and took the opportunity to add the stricken Moody's to its ranks in 1962. So, under the D&B umbrella sat both Moody's and the National Credit Office, both controlled by a culture of provided 'service'. This is an important aspect to remember.

This brings us to the 1960s. There are several aspects we need to pick apart to understand the order of things in this transformative decade. Firstly, let us consider the concept of commercial paper and the marketplace it supported. Definitionally, commercial paper is, or are short-term unsecured promissory notes issued by companies, with both the term of the paper and its security being key factors in understanding the riskiness of the vehicle. According to a Congressional investigation after the collapse of Penn Central, the commercial paper market in the mid- to late-1960s was experiencing 'phenomenal growth', with total issuances by year rising from 227 in 1967 to 615 in 1970.[7] The same investigation estimated that the total commercial paper market was worth $40 billion at the time. There were two distinct parts of the commercial paper market at the time, including both lender to borrower and also through established dealers, of which there were seven major dealers; the largest of which was Goldman Sachs. Whilst direct commercial paper deals had many advantages, 'direct paper typically offers a lower interest rate – by one-quarter precent – and most direct issuers do not have the same ability to reach purchasers as do the large commercial paper dealers, who more actively solicit purchasers'.[8] Hudson's earlier view regarding investors relying on brand reputation could perhaps be derived, albeit incorrectly, from the understanding that:

> since Goldman, Sachs is the oldest and largest dealer in commercial paper, most customers believed that Goldman, Sachs would offer them only commercial paper which met their requirements and which Goldman, Sachs felt was credit-worthy. This impression was created in large part by oral representations made by Goldman, Sachs personnel and by written materials (pamphlets and brochures) distributed by them which extolled Goldman, Sachs as the 'largest' and 'most important' commercial paper dealer.[9]

It would be incorrect of Hudson to derive his view from Goldman's assertions, simply, because of the following statement in the investigation, regarding how Goldman convinced investors to purchase commercial paper through them:

> Further enhancing this image were representations made by Goldman, Sachs that commercial paper is the equivalent of Government securities in terms of safety, that Goldman, Sachs only offered the paper of the top companies; that it maintained a credit department to review commercial paper issuers, that it offered investment advice to purchasers; that it purchased the paper of 'outstanding' companies for resale to investors; that it would provide financial information on issuers whose paper it was offering for sale; and *that it only offered paper rated 'prime' by NCO, an independent credit rating service.*[10]

It is here that one sees the error of the accepted narrative. Goldman's words are just words for the investors; it is the inclusion of an *independent third-party* that provides its top form of verification that seals the deal for the investor. In fact, the Congressional investigation went much further in demonstrating this reality.

The excerpt above suggests that Goldman enticed investors with claims of market superiority *and* the inclusion of prime ratings, but the reality is that 'the dealers utilised NCO ratings as a marketing tool in offering commercial paper to their customers since *many customers, particularly nonfinancial institutions, were required by statute or resolutions of their boards of directors or trustee, to purchase only that commercial paper which was rated by NCO, then the only national commercial paper-rating service'*. This revelation automatically kills any argument that investors relied on brand reputation alone, and sheds a different light on why rating agencies were suffering in a marketplace dominated by the usage of commercial paper: the NCO had no competition! S&P did not start rating commercial paper until 1969 and then it was only the mid-1970s when their offering became substantial, and D&B had no interest in diluting the marketplace with two of their departments (Moody's being the newly-acquired other department) operating in the same field.[11]

The Congressional investigation was unequivocal in its findings: the NCO 'contributed to the misleading of investors'. They continue by saying that the 'NCO had been rating commercial paper since 1920 and prior to 1970 it was essentially the only national commercial paper rating service. NCO was never registered with the Commission as an investment adviser'. Essentially, we have a case of an experienced and seemingly reliable entity providing critical assistance to the sale of financial products without being regulated, in the slightest. It is a theme that we will come back to momentarily. NCO had a rating scale that divided the creditworthiness of the commercial paper into five categories: Prime; Desirable; Satisfactory; Fair; and No Rating. Another aspect that I would like you to consider as we move along is the following excerpt:

> As a standard method of operation, NCO would enter into a subscription agreement with the prospective issuer of commercial paper wherein the issuer would agree to pay an annual fee to NCO for appraising commercial paper and pursuant to which NCO agreed to evaluate and assign on of the classifications to the subscriber's (i.e., the issuer's) commercial paper . . . additionally, the issuer agreed to 'furnish promptly to NCO pertinent financial reports and other data normally provided to line banks, in order that NCO may accurately appraise the commercial paper'.[12]

What the above reveals for us are two distinct realisations. The first is that for any analysis that suggests that credit rating agencies magically moved to the issuer-pays remuneration system on a whim, the proof is clear that the NCO was leading the way in that regard. The second comes with regard to one of the key arguments of the benefits of the issuer-pays system, in that the agency is supposed to have access to non-public and potentially sensitive information, thus alleviating the informational asymmetry problem but also providing the issuer with protection in signalling this potentially sensitive data to the market; with the NCO and its issuers, the NCO was receiving the very same information that many of the investors were receiving from the issuers – a fact recognised by the Congressional investigation.[13]

In trying to understand the breadth of the growing problem we are learning about, the constitution of the investors is helpful to know. For example, of the

651 outstanding ratings the NCO had at the time of the Penn Central collapse, 262 were industrial companies, 166 public utilities, 106 finance companies, 50 bank holding companies, 49 mortgage finance companies, 11 insurance companies, and 7 transportation companies; it is not difficult to see why failings in this area of commercial paper could have systemic consequences, and so it proved. Furthermore, this threat is enhanced when we consider that the NCO's ratings were the *only* safeguard in place for investors. Finally, to accentuate the position that the marketplace was in, by mid-1970 of those 651 outstanding ratings from the NCO, all but 34 still carried the full 'prime' rating, suggesting an alarming amount of 'rating inflation'. The fact that the President of NCO understood and acknowledged this alarming level of reliance makes what happened next all the more incredible:

> Mr Eugene Schenk, the president of NCO, has stated: 'NCO is the agency on which virtually all prospective buyers rely for ratings in the commercial paper field. Through the years our authoritative appraisals have been of material assistance in making a market for these short-term notes'.[14]

One may be under the illusion that, if a company is the clear 'market-maker', understands that everybody relies upon them, and that they have a unique role to play in the protection of systemically-critical industries, then the company and its parent would devote substantial resources to both maintaining and advancing the 'service' they provide. In reality, quite the opposite was true.

The Congressional investigation, based on the work of the SEC, was damning for D&B. They concluded that 'it would seem apparent from the foregoing that NCO's commercial paper department was relatively disorganised and of scant importance in the D&B corporate complex'. They reached this conclusion because of several key aspects. The first is that, prior to 1969, the head of NCO's commercial paper department was an Allen Rogers, who had only been physically present in the offices of the NCO twice in four years because of illness, and the whole team consisted of between three and four people at any one time. Upon Rogers' retirement, Rudolph G. Merker was assigned to be in charge, which was a curious decision given that he had never been involved in commercial paper rating, had no college education, and was not a chartered financial analyst. When questioned about this lack of experience, Rogers confirmed that (a) he was not told why he was selected, (b) he was not informed as to his responsibilities, and (c) he received no training or support for his role, and was essentially left to learn the job while on the job. The investigation noted, quite rightly, that with the rate of issuers rising rapidly, the department within the NCO was completely unable to fulfil its stated duties.

Such a small team, especially when so inexperienced, becomes immediately suspectable to the concept of capture, particularly when they are dealing with a select few clients. This was precisely the situation with regard to the relationship between the NCO and Goldman. Goldman would insist that any issuer it represented needed a Prime rating from the NCO, and Merker was in constant contact with leading figures within the relevant department at Goldman, specifically a man named Jack Vogel. The true power balance in this relationship would come to light towards the end of 1969.

The increasing rate of commercial paper issuance brought with it a natural deterioration in standards. This is very much predictable. However, this was a 'condition that largely went unnoticed in the inflationary environment of the late sixties', and whilst the rise in paper rates that ensued brought with it questions, the NCO responded emphatically by telling the marketplace that: ' "the market's growing exclusiveness" and "the ready availability of top quality paper, coupled with financial problems of a few finance companies, has tended to weed out lesser rated paper and many smaller firms have dropped out of the market" '. But, as Schadrack and Breimyer correctly note, 'the confusion of corporate size with liquidity tended to mask some deterioration during this period of the quality of commercial paper outstanding'.[15] In fact, post-collapse court cases would find that the NCO had no idea of the underlying risk to the issuances they were rating.[16]

In June 1969, a *New York Times* article BY Robert Metz as part of his 'Market Place' column had showcased an unfavourable view on Penn Central, which prompted Merker to speak with Rogers as he tended to do to seek advice. Merker followed this up by reviewing the Moody's Transportation Manual which indicated declining profits at Penn Central on a consolidated basis, and an overall loss for the holding company above it. On this basis, Merker spoke with Jack Vogel at Goldman who immediately told him that he was not concerned by the news. When quizzed by the SEC as part of the Congressional investigation, Merker stated that he believed in what Vogel said, saw no reason Vogel would lie to him despite being informed of the many conflicts of interest, and amazingly stated that he did not recognise any such conflicts of interest, despite Goldman being Penn Central's dealer for commercial paper. As a result of Vogel's words, Merker did nothing. However, in February of 1970 when things appeared to be getting worse, it would be Rogers who would phone Vogel on the NCO's behalf and ask, bluntly, whether Vogel saw any reason in the data that Penn Central should not be rated as Prime and whether Goldman had any plans to sell its position; Vogel replied no and Rogers said that he would continue the Prime rating as a direct result of Vogel's actions.

What Vogel did not tell Merker or Rogers was that, at the same time, Goldman had sold any commercial paper it had and was actively advising prospective clients to read the financial data at Penn Central. Remarkably, given that the NCO had access to the very same data that Goldman did, earnings announcements were ignored or missed and, even up to May of 1970, NCO maintained its Prime rating; in April, Penn Central had announced a first-quarter loss of

$17 million, with the holding company announcing losses of $62 million. The NCO only became aware that Penn Central's redemptions of commercial paper were exceeding sales *when reading the Wall Street Journal* on May 27th, which was also twelve days after S&P had downgraded the bond rating of the Penn holding company after it tried to issue a $100 million debenture. Even the day after the S&P downgrade, Merker spoke with Vogel, asked him if he still felt the same way and when he said yes, Merker committed to keeping the Prime rating intact. It was not until June 1, 1970, when Merker could no longer get information from Goldman did he pull the rating of Penn Central by suspending it, and only three weeks later Penn Central filed for bankruptcy, holding a record $82 million in commercial paper.

The reasons for Penn Central's collapse were many: subpar track conditions, years of deferred maintenance, derailments, slow operating speeds, high operating costs, poor service for supply chain purposes, and a dysfunctional management structure have all been highlighted as reasons for the demise of one of the country's largest railroad companies. Daughen and Binzen neatly summarise the effect of the bankruptcy:

The wreck of the Penn Central reached far beyond railroads, challenging deep-rooted and basic assumptions of American corporate life. This single bankruptcy caused the nation and its business and political leaders to take a fresh look, not only at railroads, but at mergers in general and, more important, at the future of the country's transportation industry. The collapse of the Penn Central raised questions about conglomerates and the diversification programs; about the role of boards of directors and how they function, or fail to function; about the inherent conflicts of interest that arise as a result of incestuous, interlocking directorates between financiers who supply money, managers who borrow the money, and brokers who traffic with both; about the relationship between big government and big business. And about the condition of American capitalism.[17]

Interestingly, the role of third-party answers to informational asymmetry also came under scrutiny from the systemic questioning that arose from the wreckage of Penn Central.

In the aftermath of the bankruptcy, Dun & Bradstreet's reputation and reliability took a public battering. The NCO took the brunt of the public criticism, rightly so, but D&B by proxy also took quite the hit and it represented, one argued, the first time that D&B had been so publicly criticised.[18] Moody's, alongside S&P, had publicly downgraded the holding company's credit ratings relatively early, which went in their favour in the new public crucible of opinion. This, then, had all the capacity to become a 'watershed moment' for the credit rating agencies, if they could navigate the choppy waters successfully.

3.3 Credit Rating Agencies Take Advantage

In August 1971, the commercial paper department within the NCO was trans-ferred to Moody's by D&B, with the NCO essentially dying as a result.[19] With the NCO name being irrevocably connected to the Penn Central collapse, the move was an inspired one. Moody's immediately changed the rating symbols to ostensibly differentiate its offering from the defunct NCO's,[20] and the effect was almost immediate: research quickly found that the standards within the commer-cial paper market, from a rating perspective, improved considerably.[21]

In the early 1960s, the Xerox Corporation has gone to market with a photocopier – the Xerox 914 – that became ever more popular as the 1960s con-tinued, providing a clear threat to the bottom line of the rating agencies.[22] The ability to sell reports to investors was about to end, given that they could easily be copied, replicated, and moved around investors for free – a concept known as 'free riding'. This has been put forward as one potential reason that the credit rating agencies changed their remuneration model, but as we have seen in the previous sector it is essentially down to a perfect storm; the demise of a market leader (NCO), the growing need for issuers to signal their creditworthiness to the marketplace, and the oligopolistic structure of the rating industry which allowed for a concerted altering of the remuneration process. However, there needed to be other components in place if this alteration was to stick.

S&P actually broke the mould first, applying the issuer-pays model the NCO had used for years, but in the municipal bond market, with Moody's joining just a year later.[23] Yet, it would be Moody's that would launch the issuer-pays model in the open corporate bond rating market, with S&P joining in from 1974 onwards. Interestingly, as a quick aside, this very brief moment in history where the rating agencies differed in their remuneration models provides with a unique insight into the potential effects of the remuneration model on credit rating standards, approaches, and arguably culture. Jiang et al. were the first researchers to con-duct this experiment, and they came to a very telling conclusion:

> In this study, we examine whether charging issuers for bond ratings is associ-ated with higher credit ratings employing the historical setting wherein S&P switched from an investor-pay to an issuer-pay model in 1974, four years after Moody's made the same switch. Many commentators and policy makers claim that charging bond issuers for ratings introduces conflicts of interest into the rating process. For corporate bonds issued between 1971 and 1978, we find that, for the same bond, Moody's rating is higher than S&P's rating prior to 1974 when only Moody's charges issuers. However, after S&P adopts the issuer-pay model in July 1974, the evidence indicates that S&P's ratings increase to the extent that they no longer differ from Moody's ratings. Because we use Moody's ratings for the same bond as our benchmark, we can con-clude that this increase in S&P's ratings is not due to general changes affect-ing bond ratings. Further, cross-sectional analyses show that S&P's ratings

increase only for bonds with greater potential conflicts of interest under the new revenue model, i.e., for bonds that likely pay higher fees or have greater incentives to attain a higher rating. These results are consistent with bond issuers gaining bargaining power when they pay for ratings. The magnitude of the increase in S&P's ratings is approximately 20% of a rating grade, which is associated with a reduction in yield spread of roughly 10 basis points in our sample. This translates into interest savings of $51,000 per year in 1974 or over $222,000 in 2010 inflation-adjusted dollars. These findings are robust to various event windows and apply to bonds in various rating categories and to senior, versus subordinated, bonds.[24]

Other research has found that this increase in rating may be because of an increase in the amount of information that flows between issuer and credit rating agency under the issuer-pays model,[25] but the inference of rating inflation remains. The suggestion had been put forward (admittedly by agents of the credit rating agencies and Moody's in particular) that rating agencies decided to change the remuneration model because it had become a public good in light of the collapse of Penn Central, especially when combined with the development of the Xerox machine, but others have rejected this assumption, saying instead that 'that credit rating has effectively become a pure public good, is more the *consequence* of charging the issuers, than it is the *cause*'.[26]

This issue of the role and the utility of credit ratings, conceptually, was of deep importance in the early 1970s. We have heard already how there was a systemic shock at the collapse of the commercial paper market, as well as deteriorating standards in the centrally-important transportation network. The effect of the demise of the railroads, philosophically, could have on the US with its particular history rooted in the railroads cannot be underplayed. That systemic shock led the way for systemically-focused responses, on top of the wide investigations into the financial issues the economy was suffering from. As the so-called 'information age' started to appear into view, financial regulators sought to inject some level of authority into different areas of the financial sector, but there is an issue with that endeavour: financial regulations often have very unintended consequences, and in the shape of the credit rating agency we get our first glimpse into how such an industry can become baked into the very fibres of a particular economic structure.

It is difficult to get an understanding of what took place within the SEC from the literature, because a large swathe of the literature is blighted with the misunderstanding regarding the trajectory of the agencies (the correction of which has taken place in this chapter). For example, Smith and Wright, quoting White, say that:

According to White, the 1975 SEC regulation extended a rule that the government had previously applied to banks to cover the nation's broker-dealers, a category of firms that included major investment banks, retail brokerages, and securities houses. In explaining why the SEC introduced this regulation in 1975, White observes that the surprising 1970 bankruptcy of Penn Central ended a long period during which few major American corporations had defaulted. A wave of broker-dealer failures had further highlighted the importance of risk-weighting broker-dealer asset portfolios. He speculates that the SEC officials responsible for the 1975 regulation must have been worried that a new bond rating agency might appear that would certify low-quality securities as investment grade. To prevent the rise of such a bogus rating agency, the SEC modified Rule 15c3-1 in 1975 so that broker-dealers could only use ratings produced by 'nationally recognized' bond rating agencies.[27]

Similarly, the scholars cite Partnoy when they say that:

Frank Partnoy stresses the importance of the 1975 regulatory change, arguing that the regulatory license the SEC granted effectively cartelized the bond rating industry by creating regulatory barriers to entry. The informational value of the ratings could therefore plummet, and indeed did, leading to multiple crises culminating in the GFC. Partnoy attributes the usually high profit margins of the NRSROs to regulation.

There has been, as we seen earlier, contrasting research that suggests the informational value of the ratings went up during the 1970s.

Nevertheless, we need to understand the SEC's decision in 1973 to understand what it meant for the rating agencies. Before that though, it is worth remembering the opposing arguments that dominate this niche field of understanding credit rating history better, the Partnoy-held view that the SEC simply decided in 1973 to cement the rating agencies into the regulatory framework, and the Flandreau-held view that regulators (and judiciary) simply respond to market practice and try (not always successfully) to formalise particular market practices with the hope of injecting some authority and control. The SEC was borne out of the same raft of regulatory changes that gave the Comptroller of the Currency the authority to enforce that certain market participants had to use rating agencies' ratings to determine their actions (certain banks and their capital buffers, etc.):

Section 4 of the Securities Exchange Act of 1934 created the SEC in the wake of the Pecora Hearings, which had convinced many Americans that existing securities regulations, including state 'Blue Sky' laws and the self-governance systems of the New York Stock exchange (NYSE) and other exchanges, insufficiently protected retail investors.[28]

Section 8(b) provided the newly-developed SEC with the authority to limit the ratio between broker-dealer indebtedness and their 'net capital' in an attempt to prevent the inability to meet obligations during a crisis, but it took the SEC eight years to bring about such a rule; the rule stated that broker-dealers indebtedness could not exceed a ratio of 20:1 'and specified that some classes of assets should be counted at less than their face value, a risk-weighting practice known as a "haircut"'. A 'haircut' is, essentially, a buffer to cover the risk of not being able to sell an asset at its current value that has been put up as collateral on a loan. The percentage of that haircut will vary, but it has to be sufficient enough to protect the lender. The SEC, for thirty years, independently determined the level of haircut needed for certain classes, and only exempted certain exchanges (like NYSE) because they instituted rules for broker-dealers using the NYSE that were much more stringent than the SEC was mandating.

It was the stock exchanges that utilised credit ratings initially. In 1929, the NYSE implemented the first iteration of a rule that would be amended several times, which:

> mandated that its member broker-dealers determine haircuts using bond ratings assigned by 'any of the nationally known statistical services'. In 1971, the NYSE modified its rule book by specifying that in following Rule 325 exchange members should use the ratings of 'Standard & Poor's, the National Credit Office, or any nationally known rating agency recognised by the Exchange'.

However, these rules were not widely enforced because of an existential crisis that affected broker-dealers, with over one hundred dealers ceasing to exist in the late 1960s which led to Congress enacting the Securities Investor Protection Act of 1970. On the back of that legislative interjection, the SEC endeavoured to make changes to its rules on broker-dealers and in 1971 announced that changes would be coming because 'individual investors needed to be better protected in the event of broker-dealer insolvency'. As the SEC continued with its plans, the NYSE urged the SEC to instil its own Rule 325 across the board, bringing rating agencies into the fold formally. Responses from smaller brokers bemoaned the potential of increased compliance costs, but associated networks supported the injection of ratings into the calibration procedures.

However, at the same time, the public profile had been rising. Whilst we today (on the whole) tend to differentiate between the reporting and rating industries, in the early 1970s this was not the case, and prominent officers within the SEC were massively concerned about the prospect of injecting credit ratings into the system so soon after the National Credit Office had performed so woefully in the Penn Central debacle. Similarly, as Moody's and S&P had just shifted their remuneration model in the field of municipal ratings, headline-grabbing downgrades of Trenton and New York City caused further unease about the prospect of formalising the use of credit ratings. Congressional hearings on the role of rating agencies, particularly in the municipal space, heard that ratings were 'subjective', 'produced by firms with insufficient manpower and computer resources', and ultimately 'unfair' towards municipal borrowers; prominent Congressman like John Murphy of New York 'demanded regulation' for the rating agencies.[29]

Yet, the business case for injecting the ratings into the system was strongly put forward by established members of the marketplace. In spite of this, after the consultation period closed, there was a distinct unease within the SEC about the prospect of injecting ratings, with a number of members supporting the concept of using market-based methodologies instead of the ratings, like 'mark-to-market', for example. Nevertheless, in November 1973, the SEC promulgated the amendment to Rule 15c3–1, and it included the injection of the ratings of nationally recognised rating agencies, just like the NYSE's rule. It also stated that at least one rating organisation's ratings should be used. However, after consultation with the marketplace, the SEC finalised the Rule in 1975 and now instead mandated that at least two rating organisations' ratings be used. Which credit rating agencies had not been determined by the SEC, but in a 'no-action letter' to Lehman Brothers in 1976, they confirmed that the Big Three of S&P, Moody's, and Fitch all constituted nationally recognised rating organisations: the birth of the Nationally Recognised Statistical Rating Organisation (NRSRO) had taken place.

It was not all plain sailing for the rating agencies, though. Whilst it is true that the ratings of the agencies became immediately more important in the wake of the SEC's formalisation,[30] and that this triggered an array of regulatory and legislative interventions that also injected the ratings into different parts of the economic framework (like banking and mortgage sectors),[31] the rating agencies were now being propelled into the spotlight more and more, which is something they did not court nor enjoy. In 1976, Moody's Executive Vice President Jackson Phillips and S&P's President Brenton W. Harries were called before a Congressional Committee, specifically relating to their rating of New York City which, despite a high rating, had just defaulted. This is in addition to other municipal rating failures, like the massive slashing of Cleveland's credit ratings in quick succession. The publicity brought Moody's (and S&P) out into the open where their secretive approach to conducting business gave their opponents all the ammunition they needed with which to attack the concept of a rating agency. In a *Washington Post* article in 1978, the author of an article reviewing the municipal ratings issue said:

It is also a somewhat secretive affair. No one on the outside really knows for sure exactly what goes on inside. And the raters prefer it that way. They will tell you in a general way what factors they consider important in evaluation of companies and governments – things like debt levels, revenue streams and growth prospects. They will even hint at how some of these factors are weighted. But they won't give you the formula, for a very simple reason: There isn't any.

'We have no such thing as a weighting system', said Jackson Phillips, Moody's executive vice president. Ratings are usually judgment calls, a mix of factual data and gut feel – which is a fact of life that doesn't do much to calm critics who allege that the agencies are overly subjective and irresponsibly capricious. In response, the raters say you just have to take them on faith – that even if they wanted to, they couldn't explain all that goes on in decided a rating. It's all, well, sort of mysterious.[32]

The Congressional committee tried to take things further, suggesting that the catalogue of rating failures meant that things needed to change. They first suggested that the SEC become an appellate court of sorts for municipal borrowers who could appeal against what they saw as unfair ratings, a suggestion which the SEC were quick to oppose on the basis that they did not want to be intervening in such matters. A more radical proposal was for the establishment of a 'federal rating agency', complete with a 'central type of bond system'; unsurprisingly in the 1970s' US, such ideas were shot down as un-American and potentially socialist in nature. Despite all of the criticism, the rating agencies continued on.

The reality of the NRSRO designation needs attention. Whilst it appears that the SEC had attempted to place themselves, formally, within a market practice by being the arbiter of such a designation, in reality the SEC were nowhere to be found. In the years between 1973 and the Global Financial Crisis, the SEC did not once explain or determine what it meant to be an NRSRO. There were no qualifying standards other than being 'national recognised' which, once the designation was set, meant you were either in the club, or out; one could not become nationally recognised without first being nationally recognised. Writing in 1996, Gerald Miller made another good point:

In reality, however, despite the importance of rating agencies and ratings to the securities markets, the commission receives little information about the rating agencies and their operations. Often the division (Division of Market Regulation) receives only informal information about the rating agencies, usually through business publications or from competing rating agencies. For example, the division learned about McGraw-Hill Inc.'s, S&P's parent company, acquisition of J.J. Kenny Co., a brokers' broker, from a *Wall Street Journal* article.[33]

Furthermore, Andrew Fight describes how: 'for not only has the concept of the NRSRO never been defined, there is no formal training, education qualification, or professional qualification required or qualifying one to become a rating analyst'.[34] Essentially, the SEC had outsourced the requirement to perform due diligence because of legislative and public pressure after the crisis affecting broker-dealers.[35]

Earlier I said that, often, regulatory interventions have unintended consequences. It is surely rare and very unlikely that regulators go on to have a negative impact on their regulations on purpose. Yet, the issue becomes whether there is enough forethought being used when undertaking certain regulatory strategies. Regrettably, a lot of regulation is cyclical; by this I mean that, often, regulators are regulating from a position of crisis and in a responsive stance. The chances of unintended and often negative consequences as a result are immediately heightened. Before we conclude this chapter, the always erudite Jonathan Macey neatly summarises the effect of the SEC's actions, and we ought to remember this as we continue through the rest of the book as it will be massively important:

> The result of this regulatory morass was that issuers who wanted to sell their securities had no choice but to pay for ratings, because if their securities did not have ratings, few if any investors would be legally eligible to buy them. In this environment, quality quickly became irrelevant. Credit rating agencies could increase profits not by raising quality, but by cutting costs. One way to cut costs, of course, is to offer lower, less competitive salaries, hiring cheaper, less competent or well-credentialed personnel . . . another way to cut costs is to invest less in technology and information gathering. Still another way was to rely on the clients being rated to do the very modelling required to generate a rating.[36]

As we move forward through the remaining decades of the twentieth century in our story of Moody's (and rating agencies in general), it quickly becomes clear that the unintended consequences from the SEC's intervention, together with the marketplace's storied usage of the products of the agencies, was soon to cumulate in something unprecedented.

3.4 Conclusion

Moody's entered the 1960s in a decline, with the future looking very uncertain. As the 1980s started, they did so with Moody's' products being hardwired into the financial system. Despite public criticism, their products remained systemically important with the national regulator unwilling to even reference their performance. From a company perspective, fate had intervened and was shining on them. However, how they got to that point remains up for debate according to the literature.

In this chapter, we saw that, rather than fate acting kindly to them or regulators plucking them from obscurity to perform systemically-critical analyses, the reality was that nothing much had changed but for some industrial reorganisation. When the market needed to understand and *signal* creditworthiness, they went to the *combined* industry which, at that point was represented by the National Credit Office. Before that they had gone to Moody's and S&P, and before that they had gone to Dun & Bradstreet, who came after the Mercantile Agency. It is a lineage defined by the market, not by the regulator or the judiciary. This is because of a simple, modern philosophical fact: when trust cannot be gained because of distance, it must be outsourced. The need to *signal* that trust, which is a theory I will present to you at the end of this book, is fundamental. The credit reference agencies and the credit rating agencies that followed all operate to service that need, the only differences are that at various points in the lineage the situation dictates that different characters step forward to meet that need. With regard to the SEC in the 1970s they were, as arguably all regulators do, *responding* – they were not making a market. That market, for haircut ratios for broker-dealers, had begun privately in 1929, so forty-four years earlier.

The issue with the misunderstandings I have presented to you in this chapter, and hopefully resolved, is that it allows for narratives to be established which are not eventually helpful. The narratives of 'regulatory licencing' have led to calls to extinguish the rating agencies all together, which is a squandering of vital thinking and resources on an eventuality that will never materialise because, quite frankly, it cannot. What the rating agencies offer is not informationally nourishing nor free of conflict or fault, it is merely *necessary* within the economic system we have – no more or less. Benjamin Taupin says that 'paradoxically, the role of credit rating agencies has been reinforced with each rating crisis',[37] and one of Frank Partnoy's most celebrated pieces of work is called 'The Paradox of Credit Ratings' but, the concept of the rating agencies' successes being paradoxical is based on the understanding that they do wrong but do not get penalised for it – there must be a reason for this. Some of the suggestions in the literature as for those reasons we have covered but, I put it to you, the reader, that it is simply because there is no viable alternative that ticks the necessary boxes for the marketplace that the agencies do. That reality was on display in the 1970s, but as we shall see next when we look at the turn of the century and what followed, it is perhaps the only answer that makes sense.

Notes

1 Frank Partnoy, 'The Siskel and Ebert of Financial Markets? Two Thumbs Down for the Credit Rating Agencies' (1999) 77 Washington University Law Quarterly 619, 648.
2 ibid.
3 Robert Hudson, Alan Colley and Mark Largan, *The Capital Markets and Financial Management in Banking* (Routledge 2013) 175.
4 Daniel Cash, 'Credit Rating Agency Regulation Since the Financial Crisis: The Evolution of the "Regulatory Licence" Concept' in Daniel Cash and Robert Goddard (eds), *Regulation and the Global Financial Crisis: Impact, Regulatory Responses, and Beyond* (Routledge 2021) 170.
5 Shashank Shah and VE Ramamoorthy, *Soulful Corporations: A Values-Based Perspective on Corporate Social Responsibility* (Springer 2013) 418.

6   D&B, 'History' <www.dnb.com/about-us/company/history.html> accessed 15 March 2023.
7   U.S. Senate, *The Financial Collapse of the Penn Central Company: Staff Report of the SEC to the Special Subcommittee on Investigations* (GPO 1972) 274.
8   ibid.
9   ibid 287.
10 ibid (emphasis added).
11 Kenneth V Handal, 'The Commercial Paper Market and the Securities Acts' (1972) 39(2) The University of Chicago Law Review 362–402, 371.
12 U.S. Senate (n 7) 292.
13 ibid 298.
14 ibid 292.
15 Frederick C Schadrack and Frederick S Breimyer, 'Recent Developments in the Commercial Paper Market' (1970) Federal Reserve Monthly Review 280.
16 Robin E Phelan, 'Recent Developments in Corporation, Partnership and Securities Law' (1976) 13 Bulletin of the Section on Corporation, Banking and Business Law: State Bar of Texas 2, 6.
17 Joseph R Daughen and Peter Binzen, *The Wreck of the Penn Central* (Beard Books 1999) 12.
18 Joris Gjata, 'The Private Roots and Public Branches of Regulation-by-Information: Understanding the Legal Incorporation of Rating in Finance and Accreditation in Healthcare (1900–1970s)' (Doctoral thesis, University of Virginia 2017) 168.
19 U.S. Senate (n 7) 292.
20 Gjata (n 18) 170.
21 Handal (n 11) 379.
22 Eva H Wirten, *No Trespassing: Authorship, Intellectual Property Rights, and the Boundaries of Globalisation* (Toronto UP 2004) 61.
23 Ahmed Naciri, *Credit Rating Governance: Global Credit Gatekeepers* (Routledge 2015) 18.
24 John (Xuefeng) Jiang, Mary H Stanford and Yuan Xie, 'Does It Matter Who Pays for Bond Ratings? Historical Evidence' (2012) 105 Journal of Financial Economics 607, 620.
25 Sam Bonsall, 'The Impact of Issuer-Pay on Corporate Bond Rating Agencies: Evidence from Moody's and S&P Initial Adoptions' (2014) 57 Journal of Accounting and Economics 89.
26 Katharina Holzinger, *Transnational Common Goods* (Palgrave Macmillan 2008) 57.
27 Andrew Smith and Robert E Wright, 'Sowing the Seeds of a Future Crisis: The SEC and the Emergence of the National Recognised Statistical Rating Organisation (NRSRO) Category, 1971–1975' [2021] Business History Review 9.
28 ibid 10.
29 ibid 16.
30 General Accounting Office, *Risk Based Capital: Regulatory and Industry Approaches to Capital and Risk* (DIANE Publishing 1998) 130.
31 Frank Partnoy, 'The Paradox of Credit Ratings' in Richard M Levich, Giovanni Majnoni and Carmen Reinhart (eds), *Ratings, Rating Agencies and the Global Financial System* (Kluwar 2002) 74.
32 Bradley Graham, 'Mystery Pervades Rating Agencies Bond Market Role' *The Washington Post* (8 October 1978).
33 Gerald J Miller, *Handbook of Debt Management* (CRC Press 1996) 518.
34 Andrew Fight, *Understanding International Bank Risk* (John Wiley & Sons 2004) 54.
35 For more on outsourcing regulatory responsibility see: Claire A Hill and others, *Research Handbook on the Economics of Corporate Law* (Edward Elgar Publishing

2012) 276; Ann Rutledge and Sylvain Raynes, *Elements of Structured Finance* (OUP 2010) 26; Timothy J Sinclair, *The New Masters of Capital: American Bond Rating Agencies and the Politics of Creditworthiness* (Cornell UP 2014) 44–6; Andrew Fight, *The Ratings Game* (John Wiley & Sons 2001).

36 Jonathan R Macey, *The Death of Corporate Reputation: How Integrity Has Been Destroyed on Wall Street* (Pearson 2013) 146.

37 Benjamin Taupin, 'Perpetuating the Regulatory Order in the Credit Rating Industry' in Isabelle Hault and Chrystelle Richard (eds), *Finance: The Discreet Regulator: How Financial Activities Shape and Transform the World* (Palgrave Macmillan 2012) 86.

4 Cultural Revolution, or Cultural Evolution? Moody's IPO on Reflection

4.1 Introduction

One aspect that has been operating under the narrative of the book so far is that of culture. An organisation's culture has been the focus of many studies over the years, with the field becoming well known, developed, and then applied to create new cultures or adapt existing ones. However, cultural development through the lens of a specific industry is less of a studied topic simply because many industries are far too complex to derive just one specific culture as connecting the member entities. In the case of credit rating agencies, however, this author is of the belief that we can very much attribute a specific culture to the whole industry, at least its constitutive parts in the Big Three.

This belief is held, mostly, because of the understanding that the upper echelons of the credit rating industry can be neatly described as a 'natural oligopoly'. One could even go further and describe it as a 'natural duopoly', given that the Big Three has rarely seen their market share alter over decades of business, and the 'Big Two' of Moody's and S&P hold a significant market share advantage over Fitch. Perhaps the concept of a natural oligopoly needs to be defined more before we proceed, but its effects are stark on the culture of the rating agencies that enjoy the spoils of the oligopoly. The oligopolistic nature of the rating industry is said to be 'natural' because the oligopolistic model is, arguably, the most efficient way of providing the services necessary for those who utilise its outputs. For example, an issuer does not need more than two ratings – one to signify its creditworthiness and another to provide support to the first signal – and having three to choose from means the rating agencies must stay true enough to their mandate for risk of being overlooked in that selection process. That binding pressure also gives the theoretical investor comfort in that the rating agencies would not act against the position of the investor because of the risk of being replaced in the oligopoly and furthermore, effectively, the duopoly. If there were, for example, ten credit rating agencies that each had a market share of 10% (admittedly a very crude example), the theory goes that the duplication costs and, more importantly, the distortion of the *signal*, would make the process inefficient and prohibitive for the movement of capital. That, in a very crude

DOI: 10.4324/9781003001065-4

nutshell, is why the oligopoly in the credit rating world is very much a natural one. To resolve the information asymmetry that exists, having too many chefs really would spoil the broth.

However, the reality is something very different. I will present to you an Afterword at the end of the book that explains the applicability of the concept of a *signal* but, in reality, the credit rating oligopoly is a credit rating *duopoly*, and that brings with it certain characteristics. For one, if you are a member of a natural duopoly, there are very few things you can do to take yourself out of it. If the environment which surrounds you *needs* you, then how can it punish you for wrongdoing? How can there be any restraint on you for maximising your position, even if it threatens particular parts of that very environment? In this chapter, as we move our story forward, these aspects raised come to the fore.

Our story has a number of 'stops' as explained in the introduction. There will be, as a result, elements to the wider story which are not covered as extensively as they may be in a more thorough examination (say, in a full historical study, for example). A good example of that is the credit rating agencies' contribution to the Asian Financial Crisis of the late 1990s, of which Moody's was very much a constitutive part. This Crisis is not reviewed here not out of apathy or indifference, but merely because of time pressures. The Crisis, which engulfed a number of sovereign states and revealed, for the first time, how credit rating agencies and their ratings could impact entire societies, was perhaps a lesson that went unheeded by countries that would suffer the same fate just over a decade later; a crisis that consisted of the rating agencies being slow to react[1] but then performing cliff-edge rating changes,[2] all based on the rating agencies chasing their own tails and mistakes[3] would wreak havoc across Asia and be replicated across Europe a decade later. The sovereign crises were, and indeed are, very important.

But for our story we will instead move forward just a few years in order to capture an event that would change the parameters for Moody's, both technically but also *culturally*. Yet, as you may be becoming used to at this stage of the book, all is not what it may seem. The literature is awash with references to the events we will focus on in this chapter – the decision to take Moody's public and its first test with the collapse of Enron – that paint a picture of a *change* in the culture at Moody's. Many different people attribute many different reasonings as to this change, but the vast majority tie this supposed cultural change to what would follow just a few years later with the Global Financial Crisis, which we will cover in the next chapter. But, what if what occurred was less a cultural revolution, but instead a cultural *evolution*? Would that change how we see credit rating agencies?

4.2 Enter the Sage

To take stock of where we are up to in our story so far, the turn of the millennium represents nearly thirty years after the events of Penn Central. In those intervening years, there is little to report on Moody's nor the other credit rating agencies. The oligopoly that was being built in the 1970s, and which the NRSRO designation crystalised, enjoyed the relative fruits of its labour in the years afterwards. No major crises affected the development of the industry, and times of relative economic comfort meant the rating agencies stayed out of the headlines. Similarly, and I appreciate I am using the term a lot, the *relative* lack of financial innovation during those thirty years meant that the rating agencies, essentially, 'knuckled down'. The issuer-pays remuneration system was in full swing, and corporate ratings continued to be the order of the day. Commercial paper markets had flatlined after the 1970s debacles and, whilst several financial products were developed in the intervening years, very few took hold of the economy like securitisation did in the 1920s/1930s, and the way commercial short-form paper did in the 1960s/1970s. This paragraph, of course, passes over many intricacies that purists could rightly point too but, in our story, it is the turn of the millennium that provides us with our next 'stop' on our journey.

Moody's had been bought by Dun & Bradstreet in the 1960s, and in the aftermath of the Penn Central collapse and the revelations regarding the National Credit Office, Moody's became front and centre for Dun & Bradstreet. However, even in the aftermath of the Asian Financial Crisis which revealed credit rating agencies to be complicit in creating a contagious financial crisis, the sector would welcome one of the world's leading financial figures. In 1999, Dun & Bradstreet was under particular competitive pressure as well as pressure from its shareholders to do something about its poorly valued stock.[4] In response, and in reaching out for help, investment banking advisers Goldman Sachs had put forward a plan of spinning-off Moody's as a separate entity, which it believed would generate the income that the parent company needed. At the time, Moody's was D&B's star business, and Goldman painted a picture that revolved around unlocking the pent-up value in the Moody's brand. News of this plan soon got out and, in response, the figurative blood in the water drew in, perhaps, the greatest of all the sharks. In the same year, the acclaimed 'Sage of Omaha', Warren Buffett, would instruct his Berkshire Hathaway investment vehicle to purchase Dun and Bradstreet. He did this for a number of reasons, but Mary Buffett (once Warren's Daughter-in-Law) and David Clarke spell out one of the main reasons:

A review of the SEC documents for Dun & Bradstreet in 1999 would have told Warren the following things about the economic nature of Moody's:

That Moody's was and is in the business of rating bonds and that it had 37% of the market, with Standard & Poor's holding 42%.

That Moody's had rated over $30 trillion of the world's debts.

That Moody's rated the debt of over a hundred countries.

That in 1999 Moody's had 4,200 corporate relationships.

That Moody's also had rated 68,000 public finance obligations.

That Moody's publishes thousands of pieces of credit research each year. Twenty-eight hundred companies throughout the world purchases its research on an annual basis, and there are over fifteen thousand individual users within those companies.

And that Moody's had been named the leading rating agency by Institutional Investor Magazine for the past five years.[5]

All of these facts look great, but for Buffett it was something else that attracted him to the investment. Speaking after the Financial Crisis in a testimony to Congress, Buffett said that he had invested in the company because the rating agency business was a 'natural oligopoly', which gave it 'incredible' pricing power to which he affirmed 'the single-most important decision in evaluating a business is pricing power'.[6] To obtain access to this incredible pricing power, Berkshire Hathaway purchased D&B for an eventual total, after rounds of stock purchases, of $499 million, for an average price of $21 a share for 24 million shares. D&B then announced the details of the proposed spin-off, which confirmed that:

'The separation of Dun & Bradstreet into New D&B and Moody's will allow each company to pursue focused strategies appropriate for its specific business,' said Clifford L. Alexander, Jr., chairman and chief executive officer of The Dun & Bradstreet Corporation, who will serve as non-executive chairman of Moody's following the spin-off. 'In addition,' Alexander said, 'the separation will also enable investors to evaluate the respective businesses on a stand-alone basis and to participate directly in the potential of two separate companies.'

In connection with the distribution, D&B will change its name to Moody's Corporation and New D&B will change its name to The Dun & Bradstreet Corporation. New D&B will retain the ticker symbol 'DNB' on the New York Stock Exchange. Moody's will also list on the NYSE under a ticker symbol yet to be determined.

The separation will be accomplished through a spinoff of New D&B from the Company through the distribution of all of the outstanding shares of New D&B common stock to the Company's shareholders. This distribution will take the form of a dividend of one share of New D&B common stock for every two shares of the Company's common stock held on the record date.[7]

With its 24 million shares, Berkshire Hathaway's stake after the spin-off was immediately transformed into 24 million shares in the new Moody's stand-alone corporation and 12 million shares in the new Dun & Bradstreet corporation. Over the next three years, Berkshire Hathaway would sell off his 12 million shares in the new D&B company for an average price of $30 a share, giving him a total sale figure of $360 million. The result of this is that Warren Buffett had ultimately acquired 24 million shares in the newly-public Moody's for an aggregated total of just $141 million, or $5.56 a share. As part of the procedure, those 24 million shares that Buffett shrewdly kept hold of split 2 for 1 in 2005, which meant Berkshire Hathaway held a total, at one point, of 48 million shares in Moody's and was, by far, the largest shareholder.

Buffett had, rather skilfully, acquired his primary target. The question is, why? Was it just for the pricing power and the position in the oligopoly? The reality is, as it often is, much more nuanced. The commonly held understanding is that, as a former managing director stated in his testimony to Congress after the Financial Crisis, Moody's corporate culture before the flotation resembled a 'university academic department' with the sentiment being that knowledge production was the driving force for the company's existence.[8] However, studying Berkshire Hathaway's own culture reveals characteristics that it looks for in those it invests in. Perhaps standing in equal importance to the ability to determine one's own pricing power by being part of an oligopoly, duopoly, or monopoly, Berkshire selects investments based on the ability of the management team to essentially self-govern. When asked about this after the Financial Crisis, Buffett said that if he had thought he would have to help the Moody's board with anything at all, he would not have invested. Furthermore, in his Congressional testimony, he said quite emphatically that, regarding the management of Moody's since he has been the dominant shareholder, 'I had no idea. I'd never been at Moody's, I don't [even] know where they are located'.

To some, this remarkable admission is a representation of a deeper issue with Berkshire Hathaway's approach to investment. Cunningham discusses that whilst Berkshire Hathaway is often lauded for its successes, it also carries a great cost.[9] This cost is revealed when we think about modern corporate governance, the chosen vehicle for determining the culture of modern business within modern society. Public bodies have determined that it would be inappropriate to govern every aspect of private business and that, as such, it should be the shareholders who monitor the developments at the companies they aggregately own. However, Berkshire Hathaway is notoriously hands-off[10] in its stewardship style, but many have argued that this 'scant oversight'[11] and lack of ethical focus[12] means that socially-critical businesses, the likes of which Berkshire Hathaway owns in majority shareholdings, are not being governed in a manner which would weed out bad behaviour. Giroux has called this the 'emptiness of corporate culture' with regards to which he states:

uncritically celebrated as models of leadership and celebrity icons, billionaires such as Gates [and Buffett] personify the emptiness of a corporate culture in which the discourse of profit and moral indifference displace wither the discursive possibilities for talking about public life outside of the logic of the market or a discourse capable of defending vital social institutions as public goods.[13]

Yet, with all this being the case, a conundrum is subsequently found. If it is indeed the case that Buffett and Berkshire Hathaway stay far away from the companies they invest in, then how is that, as the Congressional Report after the Financial Crisis described: 'many former employees said that after the public listing, the company culture changed – it went "from [a culture] resembling a university academic department to one which values revenues at all costs"'. Miles, in his excellent foray into the world of Warren Buffett, describes how Buffett has favoured business models that he looks for in his investments and, when he completes the investments, there are mechanisms which are deployed which get him the returns he believes the company can provide:

Such favoured business must have two characteristics: (1) an ability to increase prices rather easily (even when product demand is flat and capacity is not fully utilised) without fear of significant loss of market share or unit volume, and (2) an ability to accommodate large dollar volume increases in business . . . with only minor additional investment of capital.

Perhaps the best definition of Warren Buffett's CEO philosophy was written by Buffett himself in his 1998 'Chairman's Letter to Shareholders'. No micromanagement from headquarters. No one looking over your shoulder. Complete loyalty. Ample recognition.[14]

Dompret recounts a quite useful statement that Buffett once made that went 'culture, more than rule books, determines how an organisation behaves'.[15] This provides us with several conclusions to draw, but they cannot exist and be true all at once. We will cover the rise of a particular individual within Moody's who onlookers have targeted as changing the culture at Moody's from within shortly, but for now let us ask a couple of pertinent questions. One question could be, if the culture changed at Moody's after the IPO (Initial Public Offering) but Buffett did not even know where the company was based (he would have known), then how did that culture change but, more importantly, *why*? Did management know of companies that Buffett likes to invest in and morph into the perfect personification of that trend by themselves? Did one person, as we shall see in the official narrative, rise through the ranks and, just by chance, embody the modus operandi of other Berkshire Hathaway companies? Or, as I suggest in this book, was it something else? I suggest that the reality is that Buffett identified in Moody's, and in the credit rating industry moreover, key traits that lent themselves to what he needs from his investment. It is one thing to have a monopolistic, duopolistic, or oligopolistic position but *maximising* it is something else entirely. To build strategies, consciously, to withdraw economic rent from your position and risk your company's reputation and standing is no mean feat. In the citation above from Miles, the following sentence speaks volumes when utilised as a lens to examine the credit rating industry with: 'an ability to increase prices rather easily . . . without

fear of significant loss of market share or unit volume'. This sentence could easily be translated into can you exploit your position to the absolute maximum and
retain, in full, that position even when that exploitation leads to harm, liability, or
whatever other negative word one cares to insert at the end of the sentence. To
have the capacity to put that sentiment truly to the test needs evidence, and the
credit rating and credit reporting industries, which we have covered so far in this
book and which Buffett tapped directly into with his purchasing of D&B, provide
ample evidence that it has the capacity to carry out that mercenary mission. Penn
Central was not a disaster for the credit rating and credit reporting industries, it
was a template. As we shall see at the end of this chapter, Buffett's inclination that
Moody's had the capacity to undertake that oligopolistic mission was tested almost
immediately, and it passed with flying colours.

The cultural shift at Moody's, if there was even a distinct one at all, did not
happen by magic. It took certain individuals to move the company into a new era,
and who would tap into (as I suggest) the culture of the company's lineage. One
individual in particular makes the majority of the congressional investigations,
the majority of tabloid stories, and is almost single-handedly castigated as the vil-
lain that 'transformed' Moody's into the pernicious behemoth it would become:
Brian Clarkson. Clarkson, born in Detroit in 1956, read for his law degree at
the University of North Carolina, Chapel Hill, before joining Moody's in 1991
at the age of 35.[16] Despite this background and having no real affinity with big
data, Clarkson joined the structured finance team according to the financial press,
and more specifically the residential mortgage group as a senior analyst, according to the congressional investigations post-Financial Crisis. Promoted relatively
quickly, once the dust had settled from the IPO, Clarkson would hold the co-Chief
Operating Officer's position and be fully in the driver's seat for what was to come.

It is difficult to get a true picture of the supposed changing in the culture at
Moody's, because the varying viewpoints on offer tend to muddy the waters.
Whilst some proclaim that Moody's was 'lilywhite' before the IPO and others
pin the blame on then-Chairman and CEO John Rutherford for, alone, changing
the culture from academic to mercenary, others have disagreed and said that they
did not see 'any particular difference in culture' after the IPO.[17] Clarkson himself
said the following, which may be instructive to the narrative in this book:

> Clarkson also disputed this version of events, explaining that market share
> was important to Moody's well before it was an independent company. '[The
> idea that before Moody's] was spun off from Dun & Bradstreet, it was a sort
> of sleepy, academic kind of company that in an ivory tower . . . isn't the case,
> you know', he explained. 'I think [the ivory tower] was really a misnomer.
> I think that Moody's has always been focused on business'.[18]

Yet, if the demarcation, with respect to cultural evolution or revolution, is up
for debate, then the forceful development of the culture once Clarkson was in a

position to influence it certainly is not. There are countless stories in the congressional investigations that show Clarkson taking on the role of a 'dictator' as one testimony labelled him. Stories ranged from Clarkson openly abusing compliance personnel in public (a tell-tale sign of a changing of a profit-maximisation culture forming, usually), to him taking strategic decisions to formalise the cultural focus he determined was necessary. For example, perhaps the most efficient way to formalise a cultural change (or evolution) is to alter the parameters for success within your organisation. This is precisely what Clarkson did, with a good example being an instance in 2001 where Clarkson circulated a spreadsheet to his subordinates that listed forty-nine analysts and the number and dollar volumes of deals each had 'rated' or 'not rated'; according to the congressional hearings, Clarkson was cited as instructing 'you should be using this (the spreadsheet) in performance evaluations and to give people a heads up on where they stand relative to their peers'. Seemingly, the dye was cast, and hitting numbers and targets was the order of the day. This was continued by Clarkson who would send around a monthly email detailing particular departments' monthly market share relative to the same departments in S&P and Fitch with the inference being that each department was being judged relative to the deals they were rating against other rating agencies. Furthermore, email troves revealed in the post-Financial Crisis Congressional hearings show a clear top-down focus on market share emanating from Clarkson himself.[19]

Before we continue, it is worth pausing to reflect on how this was possible. As this book is, in opposition to the accepted narrative, suggesting that what took place was more of an evolution than a revolution, culturally speaking, the concept of taking a company public is worth considering. The fortunes of the company are, overnight, tied to a completely different beast and the ability to issue stock options as rewards for performance fundamentally alters the parameters of success for employees. As Kedia et al. rightly note:

Going public allows for sharper managerial incentives relative to being a division of a publicly-listed firm For a division of a public firm, the value of equity-linked compensation is impacted by the performance of all the other divisions of that firm. In contrast, for a publicly listed credit rating agency, its stock price reflects its managers' actions more closely. Further, existing literature documents that the sensitivity of executive turnover to performance is higher for chief executive officers (CEOs) of focused, as opposed to diversified firms, and for CEOs relative to those for division heads. This evidence suggests that the CEO of a public credit rating agency is likely to face greater market pressures than the head of the credit rating division of a public firm. Testimonials suggest that this change in culture and a sharper focus on the share price was achieved through compensation and promotion plans. Before going public, Moody's executives were covered under the D&B executive compensation plan which remained in effect through December 31, 2000.

Under the plan, performance share awards/stock option payments were based upon the achievement of two-year cumulative revenue targets. Subsequent to its IPO, Moody's benchmarks for the evaluation of executive performance for years 2001 and 2002 were based on growth in earnings per share, revenue, and operating profits.[20]

We will return to the effects of market share in the next chapter when we see it play out in all its glory, but the effect of the IPO is really important.

Immediately after being floated, Moody's stock simply continued to rise and rise, leading journalists to call Moody's 'the money machine'.[21] Additionally, not only did rating shopping with the Big Three increase after Moody's IPO (likely as a reflection of their increasing push for market share and being more open to being shopped at, as well as the changing nature of financial products in the early 2000s that encouraged shopping to take place), but research found conclusively that 'both in economic and statistical terms, [we find] that Moody's was more likely to assign favourable ratings relative to S&P for new corporate bond issuances in the period after its IPO'. The inference in this statement is that corporate bond ratings at Moody's went up across the board, but closer examination tells us that, even more worryingly, 'although such relative loosening of Moody's credit rating standards after it went public is seen for all bonds, it is significantly more pronounced for corporate bonds issued by large issuers of structured finance products and by financial firms'.[22] The researchers of this particular study suggest that not only does this corroborate the testimonies within the congressional hearings that indicated a conscious turning of Moody's culture towards market share, but that it was also driven by the structured finance department headed by Brian Clarkson.

It is, without doubt, true that Moody's turned their full attention towards structured finance. However, one must be careful with scapegoating one particular person; it is very dangerous indeed. All evidence points towards Clarkson being a dominating figure in Moody's at the time, but the reality was that the whole company was on board. Speaking from the very top, Chairman and CEO John Rutherford simply said 'lenders love structured finance(!)' which dispels this myth that Clarkson took the company in a direction whilst everybody else was kicking and screaming – they were not. But, if we are looking at the situation from the standpoint of attempting to understand the reasoning and methods of such a transformative culture shift, everything is pointed towards a split narrative once more. The accepted version is that Brian Clarkson almost single-handedly changed the culture and that this was all related to the presence, even if in a direct manner, to Warren Buffett and Berkshire Hathaway. In reality, as if often the case, things are much more subtle than the understanding above. The reality is one of Buffett identifying within Moody's a specific trait that it, its earlier iterations, and those that preceded its founding idea, all demonstrated whenever the opportunity arose: they would take maximum advantage of their position if and when the environment allowed. This, in essence, must be remembered at all times because the statements from those attached to the company around the turn of the millennium, after the fact, range from scapegoating to blaming to appearing to be victimised (as we shall see shortly), all of which are very much human characteristics in this situation but can either be absolutely valid or absolutely disingenuous depending upon where you stand. Let us not forget, for all this changing of culture in apparently a very significant and telling manner, very few people left. Other companies have experienced potential culture changes and instantly backtracked because of people voting with their feet – this did not happen at Moody's.

Nevertheless, the time period between D&B's ownership and Moody's going public is a hugely significant moment in time for Moody's. Whether or not it was a cultural evolution or revolution, it was certainly a cultural event and its impact determined what came next. Almost immediately, Moody's was elevated into the headlines because of what happened a year later, but if Moody's was to think that would be the height of their public shaming, they would need to think again, and fast.

4.3 The Rating Agencies Are Introduced to the Public: The Failure of Enron

Now of course the rating agencies were known to the public before 2001. However, they were not the content of public, sometimes front-page headlines before. Certainly not Moody's who, for the majority of its existence, had operated quietly and usually happily in the background. The largest rating-associated failure up to that point was the National Credit Office with the collapsing of Penn Central and, fortunately for Moody's, even being under the same parent company did not tar its name like it did for the NCO. However, that was about to change and then some.

I will not review the collapse of Enron too much here other than key facets for our story, mostly because it has been done exceedingly well by others.[23] However, Enron – a major American energy and commodities company formed from a merger in 1985 – sensationally collapsed and filed for bankruptcy in late 2001, leaving global markets reeling after what was, for a time, the largest corporate bankruptcy on record. Additionally, the auditing profession which was tied closely to the firm and, naturally, its audits which turned out to be based on false information, was badly affected and lost one of its largest members (Arthur Andersen). The rating agencies, for their part, were also caught up in the wreckage and would be made to answer for their part in the failure. Yet, we need to go back to come forward.

It is often said about the SEC that they essentially ringfenced the credit rating agencies in the mid-1970s with the NRSRO designation and have thus been guilty of instituting a so-called regulatory licence. However, this paints a picture of apathy or, dare I say it, collusion with the credit rating agencies when, in fact, there is evidence to say they are perhaps not as supportive of the rating agencies as that theory suggests. In 1994, the SEC solicited public comments on the usage of NRSROs:

> because of the expanded use of credit ratings in the Commission's rules, the Commission believes that it is appropriate to examine the process employed by the Commission to designate rating agencies as NRSROs and the nature of the Commission's oversight role with respect to NRSROs.[24]

As a result of the request, which largely suggested that the SEC take formal control of the sector and also require NRSROs to register under the Investment Advisers Act of 1940, the SEC in 1997 proposes a rule in 1997 to do just that. However, of sixteen commenters on the proposed rule, *all of them* criticised the SEC. The credit rating agencies had banded together to defend their oligopoly and brought their supporters along with them. Moody's, in its response, was particularly vocal:

> NRSROs that confine their activities solely to the expression and publication of rating opinions and analyses should not be treated, or required to register, as investment advisors under the Investment Advisers Act of 1940 ('IAA'). Unlike investment advisors, NRSROs do not make buy, sell, or hold recommendations or invest the money of others. The regulatory system established for the latter under the IAA has no value in measuring the credibility or reliability of an NRSRO's ratings or any other characteristic reasonably related to a rating agency's fitness to be granted status as an NRSRO. Moreover, the proposed requirement that rating agencies be so registered would be inconsistent with the reasoning in the U.S. Supreme Court's decision in SEC v. Lowe, 472 U.S. 181 (1985), and mark the first time that the SEC had attempted to exercise broad regulatory oversight of rating agencies without an appropriate Congressional mandate.

The agency went on to make certain points about what it believed to be the relative roles of a credit rating agency and the regulator tasked with overseeing them, if at all:

> It is clearly in the best interests of the United States and the global economy to encourage the development of vibrant and healthy capital markets on a worldwide basis. The history of the past century has demonstrated that sound rating agencies promote the healthy functioning of capital markets, but also that the health of the rating sector is, in turn, dependent upon an equilibrium that is fragile and easily upset by even well-intentioned public sector involvement.

We provide a necessary service to the public in a private manner and that cannot be interfered with, was essentially the message. Moody's suggested rather that if the SEC is looking to protect investors, then it is actually the likes of Moody's that provide the best protection and they should be left alone to do that. The agency went on to prescribe what it thought the regulator should instead be focusing on, namely that pursuing the standardisation of ratings and rating methodologies would be fruitless (and moreover even harmful) and that, as a pre-eminent global regulator, the SEC should actually be deploying its resources into leading by example and protecting the agencies' freedom of speech with 'sensitivity, even-handedness, and appreciation'.[25]

Returning to the Enron debacle, credit rating agencies were caught up in the wreckage simply because, 'until November 28, 2001, the major rating agencies rated Enron's debt "investment grade". On that date, they downgraded Enron's debt to below investment grade "junk" status. On December 2, Enron declared bankruptcy'.[26] For many onlookers, associated professionals, and politicians and regulators, maintaining an investment grade rating on an entity that would collapse completely just four days later was unacceptable. At its core, and which remains a pressing issue for the credit rating agencies to this very day, is the reality that on one hand rating agencies claim to use particular time horizons for their ratings – over months to certainly a few years – when deciding their credit ratings. Theoretically, the potential for collapse, if it is to happen, should be built into a rating and reflected accordingly. To drop a rating multiple notches over the span of days is simply antithetical to the theoretical functioning of a credit rating agency, yet all three did exactly that. On that basis, they were all called to answer for their performance and decisions.

S&P simply made the claim that the failure of Enron was not a credit rating problem, but a problem of basic fraud.[27] John Diaz, then Managing Director at Moody's, testified in front of a Congressional subcommittee and placed the blame squarely on Enron, stating that:

> throughout Moody's rating history with Enron, we followed processes and practices that conformed to our established methods of credit analysis – methods that have been proven to predict relative creditworthiness. In the case of Enron, however, that methodology was undermined by the missing information upon which our ratings should have been based and the misleading information on which the ratings were, in fact, based.[28]

Diaz did not mention that the agency had been given pertinent information from Enron regarding prospective and significant write-downs that investors would have needed to know about, but simply ignored and refused to act upon. Nor did he mention that as the company was deteriorating and even journalists were breaking clearly negative stories, his analysts were not even asking questions of

Enron officials but instead merely accepting that the meek responses the officials were publicly giving about the stories.[29]

Even up until November 9th, Moody's although having just downgraded Enron to just above 'junk' had insisted on giving Enron every chance, stating that a proposed capital injection from a prospective merger (which never took place) would bring the credit rating back up. The rating agencies were not predicting the fortunes of the firm, they were in essence trying to influence them. Nevertheless, all of the rating agencies finally gave up on Enron when the merger failed to materialise and all of the banks closed their doors to Enron, and the writing was on the wall for the gigantic firm.

Despite the obvious findings afterwards that the rating agencies should have acted sooner, they had essentially dodged the bullet that the auditing industry could not. One gatekeeper subsequently underwent major surgery, whilst another was left to operate with impunity. This was despite claims that the agencies were influenced unduly by Enron – which investigations found not to be the case[30] – and that Moody's was guilty of evidence tampering and obstruction of justice, which it very much was found guilty of in 2001.[31] Though the legislative wheels were set in motion and we would see the very first pieces of legislation against credit rating agencies, anywhere in the world, in just a few short years from this point in the story, it would be far too little and definitely too late. The legislative wheels may have been set in motion but, in the structured finance field, the engine was roaring and nothing would stop it other than itself.

4.4 Conclusion

The transition from private to public brought with it expected and impactful cultural changes for Moody's. However, in opposition to the accepted narrative regarding the culture that would take hold of Moody's as it hurdled towards the global financial crisis, this chapter shows perhaps an alternative viewpoint. That viewpoint marries together with the rest of the book so far in that the aim is always to take a wider view. It is not enough to look at Moody's, say, in the late 1990s and then look at Moody's in the early 2000s and simply state that the culture changed. When examined over a longer time period, the culture was evolved by going public, rather than being witness to a cultural revolution.

When I was first introduced to the rating agencies and to Moody's going public with Warren Buffett specifically, I remember strongly thinking that Warren Buffett's success is a strong indicator of understanding the reality of the situation, given that his long-held success is, arguably, beyond compare in the modern era; he has not invented anything, nor provides a particular service like a Microsoft, Tesla, or Amazon. He has made his gargantuan fortune from tapping into *corporate cultures* that have the capacity to reach particular results. He tells us quite openly that he seeks monopolistic, duopolistic, or oligopolistic positions but that he also wants a corporate culture that is happy to press home that advantage; one without the other is not prospectively lucrative for Buffett. In Moody's he found a perfect marriage of those two components, and he has increased his wealth considerably off the back of the deal where, in effect, he almost got Moody's for free after some clever stock arbitrage. That Buffett has maintained his leading stock domination over others in Moody's is perhaps a testament to its capability of achieving the objectives Buffett initially envisaged when purchasing D&B.

If we see the turn towards market share, structured finance, and pleasing the (concentrated) market in spite of the potential harm it could cause their reputation as part of an evolution of Moody's culture and not a revolution, then everything else almost changes upon reflection. Criticism of Clarkson, mainly, is misdirected albeit very valid. The focus on the IPO as the cause of the change, instead of the facilitator of change, fundamentally affects how one understands Moody's and its impact. The similarities to what we shall see next and the National Credit Office's outright abandoning of its reputation in the 1960s and 1970s are strikingly obvious, but for one outstanding detail: the NCO had no direct competitors in the specific field that it operated in (Commercial Paper issuances) but had alternatives waiting in the wings to take over if it overextended itself and dropped out of position – the credit rating agencies. However, Clarkson, Rutherford, McDaniel, Buffett, and a lot of other people all understand, I believe, that something was different this time: there was no alternative. The market could not go elsewhere irrespective of what the agencies did. The market was, to all intents and purposes, a captured market. There is no evidence to prove the theory that this was all consciously understood by the Moody's management and controlling minds, but I put it to you that the evidence is in the scale of the abandonment of principles that we would go on to see at Moody's; the degeneration of standards at NCO in the 1960s and 1970s was made to look like child's play by what would happen in the mid-2000s.

Notes

1 Morris Goldstein, *The Asian Financial Crisis: Causes, Cures, and Systemic Implications* (Peterson Institute 1998) 19.
2 Herwig Langohr and Patricia Langohr, *The Rating Agencies and their Credit Ratings: What They Are, How They Work, and Why They Are Relevant* (John Wiley & Sons 2010) 356.
3 Guivanni Ferri, LG Liu and Joseph Stiglitz, 'The Procyclical Role of Rating Agencies: Evidence from the East Asian Crisis' (1999) 28(3) Economic Notes 335–55, 336.
4 Natalia Besedovsky, 'Financialisation as Calculative Practice: The Rise of Structured Finance and the Cultural and Calculative Transformation of Credit Rating Agencies' (2018) 16(1) Socio-Economic Review 61–84, 74.
5 Mary Buffett and David Clark, *Warren Buffett and the Art of Stock Arbitrage: Proven Strategies for Arbitrage and Other Special Investment Situations* (Simon and Schuster 2011) 81.

6   Financial Crisis Inquiry Commission, *The Financial Crisis Inquiry Report* (GPO 2011) 207.
7   Buffett (n 5) 83.
8   Financial Crisis Inquiry Commission (n 6) 207, citing Eric Kolchinsky.
9   Lawrence A Cunningham, 'Berkshire Blemishes: Lessons for Buffett's Successors, Peers, and Policy' (2016) 1 Columbia Business Law Review 101.
10 Eric G Flamholtz and Yvonne Randle, 'Implications of Organisational Life Cycles for Corporate Culture and Climate' in Benjamin Schneider and Karen M Barbera (eds), *The Oxford Handbook of Organisational Climate and Culture* (OUP 2014) 253.
11 Cunningham (n 9) 101.
12 OC Ferrell, John Fraedrich and Linda Ferrell, *Business Ethics: Ethical Decision Making & Cases* (Cengage Learning 2012) 138.
13 Henry A Giroux, *Impure Acts: The Practical Politics of Cultural Studies* (Routledge 2013) 41.
14 Robert P Miles, *The Warren Buffett CEO: Secrets from the Berkshire Hathaway Managers* (John Wiley & Sons 2003) 20.
15 Andreas Dompret, 'Culture and Conduct' in Patrick S Kenadjian and Andreas Dombret (eds), *Getting the Culture and the Ethics Right: Towards a New Age of Responsibility in Banking and Finance* (Walter de Gruyter 2016) 15.
16 Sam Jones, 'How Moody's Faltered' *Financial Times* (17 October 2008).
17 Financial Crisis Inquiry Commission (n 6) 207.
18 ibid.
19 U.S. Congress, *Wall Street and the Financial Crisis: The Role of Credit Rating Agencies* (GPO 2010) 295.
20 Simi Kedia, Shivaram Rajgopal and Xing Zhou, 'Did Going Public Impair Moody's Credit Ratings?' (2014) 114(2) Journal of Financial Economics 295.
21 Courtney McGrath, *Money Machine* (Kiplingers 2002) 58.
22 Kedia, Rajgopal and Zhou (n 20) 314.
23 For a representative sample see: Mimi Swartz and Sherron Watkins, *Power Failure: The Inside Story of the Collapse of Enron* (DoubleDay 2003); Bethany McLean and Peter Elkind, *The Smartest Guys in the Room: The Amazing Rise and Scandalous Fall of Enron* (Penguin 2013); Lucy Prebble, *Enron* (Bloomsbury Publishing 2016).
24 Securities and Exchange Commission File No. S7-23-94.
25 Moody's, *Letter in Response to Request for Comments on Proposal Set Forth in Release No. 34–39457 to Amend Rule 15c3-1 Under the Securities Exchange Act of 1934* (Securities and Exchange Commission 1998) 3.
26 Claire A Hill, 'Rating Agencies Behaving Badly: The Case of Enron' (2003) 35(3) Connecticut Law Review 1145–56, 1145.
27 ibid 1150.
28 Prepared Statement of John Diaz, 'Moody's Managing Director in United States Senate Committee on Governmental Affairs' in *Rating the Raters: Enron and the Credit Rating Agencies* (GPO 2002).
29 United States Senate Committee on Governmental Affairs, *Financial Oversight of Enron: The SEC and Private-Sector Watchdogs* (GPO 2002) 85.
30 United States Senate, *Enron's Credit Rating: Enron's Bankers' Contacts with Moody's and Government Officials: Report* (GPO 2003) 13.
31 *U.S. v Moody's Investors Service, Inc.* (2001) 01 Cr. 339.

5   Systemic Derailment

5.1 Introduction

The so-called 'Global Financial Crisis', which I will refer to as the GFC for brevity but of which the 'global' nature is questionable (especially in its origins),[1] has been hinted at throughout the book. It is, perhaps, the natural crescendo for the book given that it was so impactful, in different guises, to the trajectory of the credit rating agencies. Never before had credit rating agencies been plunged into the public discourse like in the aftermath of the GFC and, in this chapter, we shall see exactly why.

However, in keeping with the sentiment of this book, alternative understandings of what happened will be put forward. The accepted narrative is that the agencies were a critical part of the machine that brought the world to its knees and, because of that, they faced the might of the Western regulatory system. Yet, in reality, the agencies escaped relatively lightly, have become more powerful and richer since and, crucially, have become even more embedded into the fibre of the economic system *despite* stated legislative goals of doing the exact opposite. Understanding how this came to be, and the effects of that journey will be important because the accepted narrative on credit rating agencies has no answer as to why; the 'regulatory licence' principle has been, by law, removed.

Nevertheless, the era from the IPO to the substantial suite of legislative responses to the largest financial crisis in modern history is so important to our story. In many ways, it becomes the crowning moment to a story that began in the Trade Societies in England, was developed by the Baring Brothers, then commercially sculpted by Tappan, and finally skilfully applied by John Moody; the world was about to feel the consequences of having to outsource the bridging of the asymmetric gap in the modern economy.

5.2 Laying the Tracks

Continuing our rail-based theme, the tracks needed to be laid out in a precise manner for the GFC to take place. The massive wealth generation that would

DOI: 10.4324/9781003001065-5

come from fees derived from selling, packaging, and rating financial products that contained incredible amounts of risk needed to be carefully constructed. There are, in that sense, a number of developments that take place around the same time but which coalesce into making the GFC even possible, never mind likely. We shall attack them in order for clarity's purpose, and to start with we need to veer away from the credit rating industry for a moment. We covered a number of these aspects in the first chapter, but they are worth re-considering as we come to the end of the book.

Anybody with even cursory knowledge of the GFC knows that the banking sector was at the epicentre of everything. Their failures (like Lehman Brothers) and rescue made the headlines around the world. But, whenever there is a banking failure there is often a regulatory failure in the rear-view mirror and to find the regulatory failure connected to the GFC we have to go back to the 1980s and 1990s in the US. There are several theories as to why the GFC developed, and they centre mostly around either (a) banking deregulation or (b) housing policy. The two theories overlap constantly but are worth considering separately.

Critics focusing on banking and the financial sector have pointed to a small number of systemically-impactful developments during this specific time period. Starting in the 1970s, Immergluck explains how 'the primary condition' for the explosion of RMBS (Residential Mortgage-backed Securities; a pooling of mortgage debt into one security that can be divided by the risk appetite of the investors looking to invest in the security) came about because of a 'funding shortfall':

> That is, the strong desire for home ownership and the rapid escalation of housing prices created a demand for residential mortgages that the S&Ls [Savings & Loan institutions) could not meet. Wall Street firms responded . . . As investors needed to evaluate the risk of RMBS default, which is a difficult task, specialists stepped forward to provide such services. The privileged raters became preeminent providers of evaluations of the riskiness of mortgage-backed securities . . . and as investor confidence grew, so did the rating business.[2]

Immergluck gets ahead of us here, but the sentiment is clear. Once again, situational forces define the trajectory of the rating agencies, just like the explosion in the use of commercial paper did for the NCO back in the 1960s. Moving forward, Silvers describes how an increasingly de-regulated mortgage market in the 1990s was developed in parallel with an increasingly de-regulated banking system, revolving around a 'general enthusiasm for financial deregulation bred by the high-tech stock bubble, the Federal Reserve lifted the gross revenue limitation from 5% to 25%', which was closely followed by the destruction, as Silvers labels it, of the Glass–Steagall Act which emanated from the 1930s.[3] The Citicorp and Travelers merger in 1998 represented the start of an era that would be defined by the re-emergence of 'universal banking', so called because of the housing of different financial services within an integrated platform. Universal banking was outlawed because of the impact of banking entities engaging in speculative behaviour in the 1920s and 1930s but, in 1999 with the enactment of the Gramm–Leach–Bliley Act, all of that changed and the doors were opened for Universal Banks to speculate once more.

However, this understanding has many critics. Often the debate, perhaps in reflection of the modern US, is drawn across political lines between left and right but the opposition to banking blame is vociferous, nonetheless. Friedman and Kraus argue that:

Explanations that rely on lack of regulation or deregulation as a cause of the financial crisis are also deficient. First, no significant deregulation of financial institutions occurred in the last 30 years. The repeal of a portion of the Glass-Steagall Act, frequently cited as an example of deregulation, had no role in the financial crisis. The repeal was accomplished though the Gramm-Leach-Bliley Act of 1999, which allowed banks to affiliate for the first time since the New Deal with firms engaged in underwriting or dealing in securities. There is no evidence, however, that any bank got into trouble because of a securities affiliate. The banks that suffered losses because they held low quality mortgages or MBS were engaged in activities – mortgage lending – always permitted by Glass-Steagall; the investment banks that got into trouble – Bear Sterns, Lehman and Merrill Lynch – were not affiliated with large banks, although they had small bank affiliates that do not appear to have played any role in mortgage lending or securities trading.[4]

Another ardent critic of the de-regulation narrative, Charles Calomiris, argues instead that rather than contribute to the crisis, banking deregulation actually allowed a bigger crisis to be averted 'by making banks more diversified and by allowing troubled investment banks to become stabilised by becoming, or being acquired by, commercial banks'.[5] Calomiris labels this focus on banking deregulation a 'false diagnosis' elsewhere,[6] instead pointing to regulatory failure in the housing system which we will address momentarily. The reality is likely more to do with the development of risk and capacity across the financial sector as a whole,[7] but I digress.

On the other side of the debate is the role that housing policy played in contributing to the bubble. In the Financial Crisis Inquiry Commission's investigations after the Crisis, their report included a 'dissenting statement' from Peter Wallison who, via his role with the American Enterprise Institute, laid the blame squarely at the door of housing policy in the US. As part of his longstanding focus on the Government-Sponsored Enterprises of Freddie Mac and Fannie Mae (essentially government-supported vehicles that provide for financial assistance for housing purchases amongst other things), Wallison highlights several key parts of the story, as he sees them:

- The so-called GSE Act (Title XIII of the Housing and Community Development Act of 1992) was intended to give low and moderate income borrowers better access to mortgage credit through Fannie Mae and Freddie Mac;

  In the GSE Act, Congress had initially specified that 30 percent of the GSEs' mortgage purchases meet the AH goals. This was increased to 42 percent in 1995, and 50 percent in 2000. By 2008, the main LMI goal was 56 percent.

- 'In 1995, the regulations under the Community Reinvestment Act (CRA) were tightened . . . The new regulations, made effective in 1995, for the first time required insured banks and S&Ls to demonstrate that they were actually making loans in low-income communities and to low-income borrowers'.
- 'In 1994, HUD (Department of Housing and Urban Development) . . . set up a "Best Practices Initiative", to which 117 members of the Mortgage Bankers Association eventually adhered . . . Countrywide was by far the largest member of this group and by the early 2000s was also competing, along with others, for the same NTMs (Non-Traditional Mortgages) sought by Fannie and Freddie, FHA, and the banks under the CRA. With all these entities seeking the same loans, it was not likely that all of them would find enough borrowers who could meet the traditional mortgage lending standards that Fannie and Freddie had established. It also created ideal conditions for a decline in underwriting standards, since every one of these competing entities was seeking NTMs not for purposes of profit but in order to meet an obligation imposed by the government' – 'the legislation (the GSE Act) directed GSEs to study "The implications of implementing underwriting standards that (A) establish a downpayment requirement for mortgages of 5 percent or less; (B) allow the use of cash on hand as a source of downpayments; and (C) approve borrowers who have a credit history of delinquencies if the borrower can demonstrate a satisfactory credit history for at least the 12-month period ending on the date of the application for the mortgage". None of these elements was part of traditional mortgage underwriting standards as understood at the time'.[8]

Wallison's sentiment here is that it was very much governmental policy that drove the market towards a housing bubble, with an increasing push to make loans to those considered low- and moderate-income borrowers. These are also known as 'NTMs', or Non-Traditional Mortgages and, in very basic terms, lay at the heart of the sub-prime crisis. For the very uninitiated, the simplified way of thinking about the development of the housing bubble is that the amount of NTMs, and also other types of loans like NINJA loans (a slang term for No Income, No Job, No Assets) became too large as mortgage originators raced to sell mortgages regardless of the borrower's ability to repay the loan. Once those loans were fed into a larger pool by bankers who were packaging the securities and then it was all rated highly by the rating agencies, the rest was history. Once the inescapable truth of increased defaults started affecting the pool, the whole security became infected and once that spread, the sub-prime crisis took hold. Wallison summarises it neatly:

> [T]he gradual increase of the AH goals, the competition between the GSEs and the FHA, the effect of HUD's Best Practices Initiative, and bank lending under the CRA, assured a continuing flow of funds into weaker and weaker mortgages. This had the effect of extending the life of the housing bubble as well as increasing its size. The growth of the bubble in turn disguised the weakness of the subprime mortgages it contained; as housing prices rose, sub-prime borrowers who might otherwise have defaulted were able to refinance their mortgages, using the equity that had developed in their homes solely through rising home prices. Without the continuous infusion of government or government-directed funds, delinquencies and defaults would have begun showing up within a year or two, bringing the subprime PMBS market to a halt. Instead, the bubble lasted ten years, permitting that market to grow until it reached almost $2 trillion.[9]

However, whilst a number of scholars and thinkers agree with Wallison's views,[10] others have found fault with his argument. Almost all of Wallison's views stem from the mind of researcher Edward Pinto, a former chief credit officer at Fannie Mae in the late 1980s who was relieved of his duties unceremoniously which some have pinpointed as his almost-bitter views towards the GSEs;[11] further-more, Wallison himself admitted that much of what he was saying was difficult to prove.[12]

Nevertheless, whether either or both strands of development were to blame, they were developing at the same time. Deregulation in the banking sector, often the beacon for financial development and governmental-induced pressure to increase the rate of mortgages in the country, beautifully coalesced into the potential for a living nightmare. Yet, if the credit rating agencies were not will-ing to put their stamp of approval on the pooled mortgages and provide their coveted AAA ratings to the top tier of segmented sections of each pool (known as 'tranches'), then the whole system would be a non-starter.

Moody's recognised as early as 1998 that mortgage-backed securities would be a 'whole new ball game'[13] but, critically, understood something much more important. It would be strategically critical for the rating agencies to remain out-side of the purview of regulators, specifically with regard to their methodological independence. Credit rating agencies have, since they started, argued that their methodological independence is what provides the market with what it needs and this cannot be infringed, under any circumstances. This is also useful when, as we shall see, you make the methodologies up to suit your client but, again, I digress. This was why, as we have discussed, in 1994 the credit rating agencies banded together to defeat the attempts by the SEC to bring about registration procedures for NRSROs; the agencies knew, what starts with registration can quickly escalate. The rating agencies would utilise another tool at their disposal as the 2000s went on, deploying resources into lobbying endeavours to water down the impact of the very first legislation that would come their way with the CRA Reform Act of 2006 – as it turned out, the Act was watered down and was far too little and very late indeed, as the Crisis would come to a head just a few years later. I raise the concept of lobbying because it is often the 'go-to' idea when one thinks of a corporate entity applying pressure on public bodies, but it is not the only option available to a corporate entity, especially when that entity is supplying a necessary product from an oligopolistic position.

For example, something that was slightly disingenuous about the housing policy argument was that it suggested that governmental policy pushed increased home ownership on the market without any safeguards in place, which is not true. Those federal pushes were buttressed by a range of state-level endeavours aimed at preventing predatory lending, as Immergluck explains:

> Following the initial actions of a few early states, other states continued to consider more comprehensive antipredatory lending regulations. By 2003, the National Conference of State Legislatures listed more than thirty states as having passed predatory lending statutes, and by the beginning of 2007 only seven states had no sort of 'mini-HOEPA' statutes or sets of laws restricting prepayment penalties, balloon payments, or predatory practices or terms.
>
> HOEPA (Home Ownership and Equity Protection Act 1994)
>
> Many so-called antipredatory lending laws at the state level had been heavily influenced by state banking lobbyists . . . when consumer advocates and community organisations made efforts to strengthen lending regulations, they were often thwarted by industry advocates and lobbyists. Banking and financial services lobby groups have traditionally had a great deal of influence on state legislatures in the mortgage regulation arena. Moreover, federal banking laws put pressure on state legislatures to accommodate banking interests.[14]

As Immergluck suggests above, those state-level efforts were hugely affected by lobbying efforts. He follows this up by telling us that 'a key set of actors in the state-level policy debate were the GSEs Fannie Mae and Freddie Mac and the three primary credit rating agencies . . . these firms had significant leverage over state policymakers'. It is this word 'leverage' that makes all the difference and explains how the rating agencies have traditionally exerted their will in the marketplace; fortunately for them, rarely do they need to engage in something as costly as lobbying.

In Georgia in 2001, Senator Fort introduced an anti-predatory lending bill into the Georgia Legislature which was, to onlookers at the time, immediately considered to be one of the strongest anti-predatory bills in the US. Predictably, the RMBS machine went into overdrive to overturn the Bill's ascent and, in 2003, S&P led the charge – closely followed by Moody's and then Fitch – in declaring that they would not rate any securities containing mortgages based in Georgia 'for fear that some of the underlying loans might violate the Georgia Fair Lending Act'. Even though Senator Fort fought back and asked S&P's Chairman directly and publicly of the agency's relationship with lenders and originators in the state, it was too late; the Bill was quashed, and a much weaker, watered-down version took its place. The leverage had been applied with the expectant results on show for all to see. The battle became a warning to other states – nobody dared follow Georgia's lead in the future. As Reiss confirms, 'the lack of a rating from at least one of the privileged rates . . . the financial equivalent of a death sentence for a residential mortgage-backed securities offering'.[15] Reiss also makes a compelling argument which reveals to us, potentially, one of the weapons used by the rating agencies when defending their interests:

The most worrisome of the three approaches to standardisation is that of the privileged raters. The privileged raters have implemented guidelines relating to predatory lending legislature that do not accurately measure the risk that such statutes pose to investors. In particular, they exaggerate the risk posed by assignee liability and punitive damages provisions in such legislation. Ultimately, these guidelines have had two major impacts: (1) they promote the interests of issuers and investors over those of homeowners, and (2) they promote the growth of the residential mortgage-backed securities market. Not coincidentally, the privileged raters make more money in such a growing market because they charge issuers for their work in rating new securities.

There is no way to formally or informally appeal the decisions of the privileged raters. And because there is not adequate way to exercise public pressure on them, their misjudgements interfere with legitimate state policies to the benefit of the privileged raters themselves, which amounts to an abuse of the privileges that they have been granted by government regulators. The privileged raters' actions have caused some state legislatures to water down predatory lending bills under consideration and have caused others to amend and dilute existing predatory laws . . . this is because funds for loans can dry up in a jurisdiction that has enacted a tough predatory lending law that falls afoul of the privileged raters' guidelines. As this catastrophic scenario has already occurred in one state, others have quickly learned that the privileged raters have an effective veto over their predatory lending laws.[16]

The track had been laid for the financial crisis. Banking was more flexible and provided the heavyweight support to contribute to the bubble. Housing policy had pushed for the increasing of non-traditional mortgages, whilst lobbying efforts and the rating agencies' effective veto had seen off any challenge to provide guardrails at the state level. The rating agencies had also fought off any attempt to intervene in their methodological independence. All that was left to do was to pull the lever for full speed ahead and enjoy the fruits of years' worth of labour.

5.3 Credit Rating Agencies and Banks Both Shovelling Coal Into the Same Engine

As we know, the rating agencies were 'essential to the smooth functioning of the mortgage-backed securities market'.[17] However, whilst Moody's (and the other CRAs) were outwardly advertising how much they help investors, privately the game was on to please issuers of debt, and of structured securities, as much as possible. Moody's hired a consultancy firm to conduct seminars for structured finance analysts on how to 'talk to issuers', whilst Clarkson abandoned the long-standing principle that analysts were not to fraternise with issuers, instead openly encouraging socialising between the agency's staff and the issuers they were rating.[18] Yet, all was not so positive.

The relationship between the agency and the issuers contained a much darker side, with stories of intimidation and analysts being removed from their positions on the say-so of influential issuers. If an analyst was identified by the issuers as being 'difficult', they would be replaced. Ashcraft suggests that originators 'could easily arbitrage rating agency models',[19] meaning the issuer could shop between the agencies and apply pressure where they needed to (they were pushing against an open door), and Besedovsky cites Richard Michalek, a former lawyer within Moody's structured finance group who, in his deposition to the post-Crisis investigations said that Goldman Sachs, one of the leading issuers, had a specific person tasked with arbitraging the rating agencies.[20] The issuers did this for one simple reason: they needed the right ratings to sell their products. As the FCIC investigation found:

> CDO managers and underwriters relied on the ratings to promote the bonds. For each new CDO, they created marketing material, including a pitch book that investors used to decide whether to subscribe to a new CDO. Each book described the types of assets that would make up the portfolio without providing details. Without exception, every pitch book examined by the FCIC staff cited an analysis from either Moody's or S&P that contrasted the historical 'stability' of these new products' ratings with the stability of corporate bonds.[21]

Furthermore, in a scene reminiscent from the Penn Central debacle, the amount of issuers were few leading to a concentrated relationship between the agencies and the issuers. Apart from the same conflicts of interest we saw in the Penn Central example, this time the same playbook was deployed but with different results. Many of the testimonies after the Crisis pointed towards the understanding that staffing levels were kept purposively low by management and that this had a number of effects. We will cover the effects on the methodological competence at the agency in a moment, but the effects on the workforce alone were considerable. Speaking in his exit interview, Jay Siegal noted how 'staffing issues have become a great challenge',[22] whilst a former team managing director noted to the FCIC that 'my role as a team leader was crisis management. Each deal was a crisis'. This led to a low retention rate amongst analysts, with 13 out of 51 analysts in just a two-year period leaving to join the very same investment banks they were rating. Clarkson explained to the FCIC that this was because 'the banks paid more' but, worryingly, even the post-employment protections against conflicts of interests were not monitored correctly, with the FCIC finding that 'Moody's employees were prohibited from rating deals by a bank or issuer while they were interviewing for a job with that particular institution, but the responsibility for notifying management of the interview rested on the employee'. It is not hard to see why critics have said that the rating agencies joined the issuers in the 'partaking of the punch bowl'.[23]

However, all of the revolving doors and poor governance would not have mattered if the methodologies were both stringent and adhered to. For a rating agency, if the methodologies are both (a) sound and (b) adhered to, then only the intervention of the rating committee and its injection of subjectivity can throw things off course. Sadly for Moody's, all three were areas of distinct failure in the lead-up to the Financial Crisis. The FCIC note, quite remarkably, that 'Moody's did not even develop a model specifically to take into account the layered risks of subprime securities until late 2006, after it had already rated nearly 19,000 subprime securities'. Analyst emails also confirm that this remarkable situation was well known within the agency, though nobody cared to do anything about it.[24] The lack of a methodology for sub-prime mortgages, the growing core of the majority of deals, was covered up by the fact that Moody's only had one methodology for RMBS up unto 2003; in 2003, it created a new model called M3 Prime to rate Prime mortgage-backed deals, with analysts' emails noted as saying things like 'is the goal for analysts results to be the same as M3 or for M3 to be an input into an informed decision?' Quite a remarkable question when one thinks about it.

The M3 model allowed Moody's to automate the process more, which translates into allowing it to put through more deals. However, the model did not account for even the possibility of a national drop in prices and even when that started to happen in reality, Moody's refused to acknowledge it in their methodologies. According to Siegel, in 2005, 'Moody's position was that there was not a . . . national housing bubble'.[25] So, instead of seeking methodological clarity, Moody's instead continued on whatever course would allow it to rate deals as they came in. To allow for this to happen, analysts were allowed to manually update methodologies as and when to suit the issuance, and also the injection of 'qualitative analysis' to get the rating over the line was a favoured tactic by analysts and the respective rating committees which have to sign off on the ratings. Jerry Fons, when describing the problem of wilful ignorance within the rating committees, said:

> I sat on this high-level Structured Credit committee, which you'd think would be dealing with such issues [of declining mortgage-underwriting standards], and never once was it raised to this group or put on our agenda that the decline in quality that was going into pools, the impact possibly on ratings, other things . . . We talked about everything but, you know, the elephant sitting on the table.[26]

That elephant on the table was a substantial one, but nothing would get in the way of rating deals and, whilst it may seem obvious, there was a very good reason for that.

Moody's was paid per deal, and the size of the deal determined how much the agency was paid. There were caps applied to 'standard' CDO ratings of $500,000, and as much as $850,000 for 'complex' CDOs. The profit from these ratings rose from $199mn in 2000, or 33% of Moody's revenues, to $887mn in 2006, now up to 44% of revenue; from 2000 to 2006, the corporation's revenues surged from $602 million to $2 billion, and its profit margin climbed from 26% to 37%. When we think back to Buffett's deal in 2000, it looks particularly inspired when put up against those numbers. Yet, from 2007 onwards, the good times for Moody's would come to a crashing halt.

5.4 Derailment

Rather remarkably, up until 2004 the analysts who produced rating were the same ones responsible for monitoring the rating. With an ever-decreasing workforce, this situation was obviously not ideal, and downright dangerous in reality. Therefore, as late as 2004, a chief credit officer was charged with creating an independent surveillance team to monitor rated deals. That surveillance team would be called into action almost immediately, and in 2006 they began to notice a rise in early payment defaults in mortgages originating from a specific lender – Fremont Investment & Loan. That same CCO, Nicolas Weill, would write to Clarkson and McDaniel after Moody's downgraded several of Fremont's securities to say 'this was a very unusual situation as never before had we put on watch deals rated in the same calendar year'.[27] However, more was to come.

In July 2007, Moody's took the unprecedented step of downgrading 399 subprime mortgage-backed securities that had been issued just the year before, equating to more than $5bn worth of securities. Furthermore, it was not just the downgrades that caused alarm, but the scale with many downgrades representing cuts of four notches on the rating scale, and some even more. Speaking about the downgrades, Weill said that the decision was taken to 'avoid creating confusion in the market'. With S&P naturally following suit just days later (downgrading 498 deals), the market started to panic. Investment banks were keen to get the deals off of their books, which resulted in Eric Kolchinsky sending a team email around that said:

> while I understand that bankers are putting a great amount of pressure on you to respond, the other committee chairs and I are not able to sign off on every new change, spreadsheet, or mark . . . here is what I think we need to do: don't feel rushed by the bankers – we MUST get the ratings right.[28]

This request and sentiment from a committee chair is worth noting, mainly because of what came next.

The total slashing from Moody's for the 2006 securities came to a staggering 83% of all securities that were issued in 2006 were downgraded. Never before in the history of credit ratings had such a move taken place. Nevertheless, with banks seeking to empty their product portfolios any which way they could, and with Eric's words clearly in the forefront of their mind, 'the firm continued to rate new CDOs using existing assumptions'. Of the $51bn of deals that were rated after the mass downgrade, 88% of deals were rated AAA using exactly the same methodology that had just failed in the 2006 round of issuances. As an aside, I wanted to draw your attention to this paragraph specifically. Earlier, when I said that it is one thing to enjoy a monopolistic or oligopolistic position but it is another thing to trust in it and press home your advantage despite the logical warning that it will cost you your reputation, this is precisely what I was referring to. Even when some managers spoke about the usage of the failed methodology to rate deals that were suspicious, that is, putting the reputation on the line, they were 'admonished' by their superiors for even bringing it up.[29] The pedal was hard down onto the floor at this point before the incoming wall was too close to avoid.

When the bubble burst, the aftermath presented an opportunity for Moody's to deploy some age-old tactics as it knew it had to defend itself in the crucible of public opinion. The era-defining 'bail-outs' of the financial system using public funds meant that every guilty member of the financial sector was hauled up for public vilification and, as such, particular measures would need to be deployed by the agencies. The first thing they did was flood the market with 'academic' articles from members of Moody's, infiltrating scholarly debate and steering the literature towards one of an increasingly technical nature within which they felt the company would be safe. They also infiltrated the media to turn public attention away from their misdemeanours, although the media soon got tired of this and prevented the strategy from taking hold when it became clear who was in the wrong; a move which irked Clarkson:

> And it has frankly been difficult for us to control a lot of that messaging. We have had extensive outreach to the media, both in print and electronic media. I think we've had very good success with our experts, people like John Lanski and Mark Zandy. Chris Mahoney has been on at least the radio several times. I don't know if he's been invited to be on TV, but I think we've had very good outreach with our technical experts.
>
> We've frankly been somewhat less successful in controlling messages about Moody's and getting our point of view into the marketplace, and its not for lack of trying. We have reached out to all of the significant media: *New York Times, FT, Wall Street Journal, Bloomberg, Reuters*, etc.
>
> And right now, the message we are communicating about, one, the fact that we are independent and, two, that we are competent. It's not a message they really want to hear.[30]

The second thing they did was increase their lobbying effort. No amount of 'leverage' would save them from the legislative hailstorm that was coming their way and they acted accordingly. In 2009 alone, the credit rating agencies collectively spent nearly $3 million on lobbying efforts which, whilst it may not sound a lot, was a record for the credit rating industry.[31]

The world of lobbying is a particularly nuanced world, as Dyson explains:

> the boundaries between finance ministries, debt management offices, offices of budget responsibility, central banks, financial markets, lobby organisations, financial media, and academia are highly permeable . . . Not least, financial market lobbying of international, European, and domestic supervisory and regulatory institutions is intensive, discrete, and confidential. It is backed up by carefully targeted party-political donations.[32]

The credit rating agencies were certainly not alone in lobbying to protect their positions ahead of what was surely to be wide and extensive regulatory reforms, and Larry Summers himself claimed that the financial sector was funding four lobbyists after the height of the Crisis to every member of the House of Representatives, at a cost of about $1 billion. The impact was clear as the calls for stringent and precedent-setting action were attacked from all sides in the lead-up to what would be the US's flagship legislative response to the Crisis: The Dodd–Frank Act of 2010.[33]

The credit rating agencies knew two things specifically: regulators tend to follow the flow of ideas in a hierarchical manner, and that there were key battlegrounds where they could not afford to cede any ground, at all. With regards to the former point, by this I mean that financial regulators often have a template, or an order of things that they often follow, and one of the most prominent levels of the hierarchy is that which starts with IOSCO. IOSCO, or the International Organisation of Securities Commissions, usually sets the scene for regulatory and legislative developments in the securities markets, and the market is more than aware of this. This is why, in 2008 at the height of the Crisis, the credit rating agencies collectively called for a revision of the IOSCO Code of Conduct, an advisory and non-binding self-regulatory code that all credit rating agencies adopt (and, in truth, go much further beyond).[34] This set the scene of the credit rating agencies attempting to influence the debate early, as we heard from Clarkson himself earlier. With regard to the latter point, the credit rating agencies understood that there were certain things that would come to an end for them, but that there were other aspects that they needed to protect at all costs because of the effect that not doing so would have on their future. For example, the free-for-all era defined by no formal regulation at all was surely to come to an end, and there would need to be changes in terms of registration, transparency, and rating processes. However, the key amongst everything for the rating agencies was the concept of *independence*. Nothing about the lead-up to the Financial Crisis and what would be revealed afterwards in litigation (which we will cover shortly) suggested that the rating agencies were independent: they actively sided with issuers against investors. However, the *theoretical* independence that the rating agencies need to provide the *theoretical* function the markets require of them is sacrosanct and the agencies know it. This is why Clarkson was clear that the message coming out of Moody's needed to be focused on independence and all the lobbying efforts needed to focus on one thing only: making sure regulators stayed well clear of intervening, in any way, in their methodological independence. Methodologies and rating scales etc. could not be influenced at all by public bodies, or so the theory goes.

This is why, as Quaglia describes:

[T]the main credit rating agencies (Standard and Poor [sic], Moody's, Fitch, A.M. Best) lobbied to exclude provisions that in their opinion would restrict the analytical independence of the credit rating agencies. In their response to consultation, they argued that EU rules should not regulate the substance of credit ratings and the methodology used by credit rating agencies, but rather the principles and processes that a credit rating agencies follows to generate a proper rating. This was also stressed by the British and Dutch finance ministries.[35]

The rating agencies, as well as other financial industries, utilised the increased complexity that had been injected into the financial system to their advantage, based upon a concept called 'conscious complexity'. Kwak explains that, as a result:

> The complexity of many legislative provisions, such as new derivatives regulations, played into the hands of the financial institutions and their lobbyists, who could use their technical expertise to influence the drafting process. In addition to direct lobbying, the industry enlisted support from other groups within the business community.[36]

Those other groups included so-called 'experts' like academics who provided their analytical support, for a price.

The credit rating agencies were successful, to a degree. The expected onslaught came in the form of the Dodd–Frank Wall Street Reform and Consumer Protection Act of 2010. In it, the credit rating agencies received their very own subtitle, providing meaningful and direct regulation for the first time (the CRA Reform Act of 2006 came far too late to be meaningful). The Dodd–Frank Act took aim at the exposure to liability of the rating agencies, qualification standards, rating symbols, and requested extensive official studies on the conflicts of interests inherent within the industry. The Act did three things of note. The first was to establish a bar for exposure to liability which, although it was set almost prohibitively high, was still set. The second aspect was to push to the removal of 'regulatory reliance' on the ratings of the agencies, enforcing that all federal laws and regulations remove the reference to 'ratings' and replace them with other appropriate measures of understanding creditworthiness (it is worth noting that, at the time of writing some thirteen years on, this still has not happened fully). The other aspect to note was that the Dodd–Frank Act mandated for the creation of a specialised office within the regulatory framework to deal with the monitoring and focus on rating agencies, to be called the Office for Credit Ratings to be housed within the SEC. For a period of almost three years, the OCR went unstaffed.

Of course, there were many other aspects to the credit rating-focused sections of the extensive near-900 page piece of legislation. The most important aspect, arguably, was the setting of a bar for exposure to liability which would go on to have a direct effect on the agencies, but for the most part, the credit rating agencies would have been, I suggest, quite happy with the outcome. The bar for exposure to liability was set incredibly high, with the important aspect being that a claimant had to be in a privileged position, that is, the credit rating agency had to know who would be utilising their ratings, which prevented the rating agencies from being exposed to what in the legal world is called the 'floodgates problem' (excessive exposure to liability). It also instructed that the burden of proof was on the claimant to prove the 'state of mind' of the rating agency, that is, they acted maliciously and/or should have known to do better and did not. We shall cover how that played out in reality next. Other 'wins' for the rating agencies were that the legislation stayed well away from mandating anything at all to do with the methodologies and rating processes; merely, the credit rating agencies now had to publicly disseminate their methodologies and could not deviate from them after the fact. This sounds positive until we realise that the rating committee, where all of the subjectivity and business influence can be injected into a rating, was left absolutely untouched by the legislation. Lastly, but perhaps most impactfully, the 'regulatory reliance' argument had always positioned the state as an important actor in forcing the rating agencies onto the marketplace. Now, whilst we know this was not the case, at least there was something to aim for that then had 'skin in the game' but, since the Dodd–Frank Act, this is technically no longer the case. The state, essentially, washed their hands of the whole affair thirty-five years after formally inducting them into the state's regulatory framework. It was now very much 'buyer beware', and nothing more.

Yet, the rating agencies' exposure to liability was set. Certain characteristics and instances had to be present for the bar to be cleared, and litigation started in earnest in the aftermath of the Crisis as burned investors tried to claw back what they had lost. Of particular interest is the concept of the 'Structured Investment Vehicles', or SIVs. You may also have heard of 'Special Purpose Vehicle' which is very similar, but differs in its increased flexibility whilst SIVs are specifically funded by issuing commercial paper. It is not my intention to delve into the technical like others have so adequately done,[37] but Castro's opening salvo in his excellent chapter sets the scene perfectly for us:

> It should be kept in mind, however, that every SIV is unique and there can be significant variation in the specifics of each investment vehicle. The first SIV, Alpha Finance, was established in 1988 by Citibank. At their peak in mid-2007, Moody's said there was almost $400 billion outstanding and they were rating 36 SIVs. According to a Bank of America presentation, the $400 billion of assets was funded via CP ($130 billion, MTNs (medium-term Notes) ($235 million), and capital ($35 billion).[38]

Essentially, an SIV has been specially set up to buy longer-term assets using shorter-term funding options. The SIV then 'issues to investors debt securities that are secured by the assets purchased by the SIV'. However, once the crisis had hit, the rating agencies were actively downgrading the commercial paper and MTNs that made up the majority of the assets held within the SIVs and, thus, the SIV market collapsed. Investors were, often, entirely wiped out to the tune of billions of dollars whilst the SIV was simply closed down. To try and claw back those losses, the investors went after those that had set up the SIVs, and those that had provided the ratings for the SIVs and their underlying assets. Yet, what was revealed was even worse than could have been imagined.

There are two main SIVs that hit the headlines but the majority collapsed. Taking one of those main SIVs as an example, the *Rhinebridge* SIV collapsed, resulting in losses for several investors including municipal investors like King County who would eventually go on to lead the charge against the agencies. The litigation alleged that the rating agencies had not only provided inflated ratings to the SIVs without knowing the real riskiness of the assets being held by the SIVs but were *actively* involved in the design and development of the SIVs alongside the investment banks:

> The Rating Agencies had a significantly ongoing role in the operation of Rhinebridge, which included (among other rights and responsibilities) the right to veto changes in management and the right to review and potentially veto any changes in how Rhinebridge obtained funding, modified its operating instructions, or changed its investment guidelines. Regardless of their historical roles, the Rating Agencies did not merely provide ratings; rather, they were deeply entrenched in the creation and operation of Rhinebridge. The Rating Agencies were compensated for their involvement with Rhinebridge, and had significant economic incentives to provide falsely high Ratings. Each of the three Rating Agencies gave the Senior Notes the 'Top Ratings' without which Rhinebridge could not have existed. Yet these ratings were false or misleading, in part because all three Rating Agencies used information that was stale and inaccurate, and models that were outdated. Moreover, the Rating Agencies knew that their ratings were false or misleading because they: (1) had access to confidential information about the assets held by Rhinebridge; (2) had knowledge unavailable to the public regarding the assumptions and methodologies used in rating the SIV; and (3) knew that, although the goal of an SIV is to acquire high-quality assets making it worthy of a 'Top Rating', the Rhinebridge SIV included low-quality toxic mortgage-backed assets.[39]

The investors would eventually settle with the rating agencies and investment bank in charge of Rhinebridge for an undisclosed fee (suggested to be in the hundreds of millions total). However, that was not the end of their exposure. A similar SIV called *Cheyne*, and another called *Sigma* (as well as a lesser SIV called *Stanfield Victoria*) had led to remarkable losses, and the large and influential pension fund in the US – CalPERS – was determined to get its money back. Initially, it alleged that it had invested $1.3 billion into the SIVs and that:

> the rating agencies were indispensable players in the structuring and issuance of SIV debt which they subsequently rated for huge fees paid by the issuers – 'rating their own work' according to a recent SEC report . . . the rating agencies became actively involved in the creation and ongoing operation of structured finance products like SIVs. Indeed, not only did they structure the Cheyne, Stanfield Victoria, and Sigma SIVs here in question, but they were also actively involved in the creation of the structured finance assets

held by SIVS, like RMBS and CDOs. What is more, the fees were contingent on the SIV being offered to investors. This meant the rating agencies had a contingent fee interest and thus every incentive to give high 'investment grade' ratings, or else they wouldn't receive their full fee. As former COO of Moody's Brian Clarkson said, 'you start with a rating and build a deal around a rating'.[40]

Clarkson's words had come back to haunt him.

One of the most crucial aspects to the SIVs was that 'Cheyne, Stanfield Victoria and Sigma were not available to purchase by the general investor community, but could only be sold to a specific class of investors'. These so-called Qualified Institutional Buyers were essentially systemically-important investors fed into a machine within which they were technically not allowed to know the details:

only the SIV manager and the rating agencies knew what assets made up Cheyne, Sigma and Stanfield Victoria. The exact make-up of assets was treated as confidential, lest anyone, even investors, learn CUSIP-level data of what was contained in the SIVs and be able to copy it.

This remarkable reality was, however, only one of the necessary two boxes that needed to be ticked in order for the liability bar to be cleared. The other was in proving the state of mind of the agency, and CalPERS' fortitude to go after *all* of the Big Three paid off as they essentially split the oligopoly. All three were guilty but some more than others and that pressure paid off when CalPERS settled with Fitch for their wrongdoing, but not one cent changed hands. Instead, Fitch provided CalPERS with damning information – which has never been publicly released – but must have been incriminating because, immediately, the Big Two wanted to settle. However, by this point, the Department of Justice had got involved and taken the case forward on behalf of others who had been harmed by the actions of the rating agencies. The DoJ initially was after an incredible $5 billion in damages. Quite remarkably, S&P suggested that this fervour from the DoJ was because of a historic downgrade of the US sovereign credit rating in 2011, which only seem to rile the then-Attorney General Eric Holder.

In what would be a record settlement with a credit rating agency, S&P would back down from their aggressive stance against the DoJ and settle for a record $1.375 billion in 2015, whilst also officially backtracking on their claim of an institutional reprisal for their sovereign rating four years earlier. Just two years later, the DoJ would settle with Moody's on exactly the same grounds, this time totalling $864 million. Both would also privately settle with CalPERS. In total, the Big Two would pay out more than $2.2 billion for their role on the losses of investors, with CalPERS reporting to their members that, essentially, everything that had been stolen from them they had clawed back. As part of their settlements, which are very different from penalties, the agencies were allowed to publicly admit no guilt and were barred from being chased for any more money from investors from the crisis era. I have argued elsewhere that the in the run-up to the Crisis, the rating agencies actively built consultancy services to go alongside their facilitative ratings offerings and which generate billions in profits – to a point where, at Moody's, Moody's Analytics almost brings in more than their rating business – so, in reality, those era-defining settlements really were not that penalising at all.[41] But, for the rating agencies, they were now able to move on and reflect on what they and others would go on to call 'legacy issues'.

In the European Union, the bloc would be forced to take a different approach to the regulation of the rating agencies given their unique exposure to the ratings as a multi-State bloc. As they were brutally exposed to the counter-cyclical ratings during the impactful sovereign debt crisis that started in 2011 and brought a number of European nations to its knees, the European Union ramped up its legislative protection by bringing in a programme of registration under a new regulator, and rules designed to implement transparency in the rating process, focusing on aspects like the timeliness of ratings, the factor of solicitation, and the transparency of methodologies. However, they still refrained from infringing or influencing the ratings in any way, shape, or form: remember, the methodological independence of the credit rating agency must not be tampered with!

I have, intentionally, skipped over a lot of the minute details regarding the regulatory developments concerning the rating agencies. I have done this for two reasons. The first is that others have so wonderfully examined every detail of the regulations that came from the US and the EU after the Crisis, and they are not hard to find. The other reason is that, in reality, those regulations matter little. The degeneration of standards was in relation to that specific time period and that particular bubble; that environment will not be replicated again in the same way. A regulator/legislator then must face two very uncomfortable truths. The understanding that the Penn Central collapse and the housing market crisis were, as far as the rating agencies' involvement, near identical, means that to stop it from happening again there would need to be systemic change, not just a change to the façade: no regulator or legislator has the capacity, authority, and I argue the will to do that. The second truth is that the legislator and regulator are philosophically in the position of responder, which means they are fundamentally always behind the curve. They cannot respond pre-emptively because to do so could easily be spun to look like they are anti-capitalist and anti-business, which a regulator fundamentally is not. If they are always operating behind the curve, the question then becomes how far behind the curve are they, and can they shorten that space? The reality, as we have seen in this and other chapters, is that the drivers of the financial developments often far outweigh the regulators tasked with supervising them in terms of resources and capability. Ratings have become more centralised since the Crisis, more intertwined, and the rating agencies have continued to transgress all whilst the regulators have tried to remove themselves from the blame of putting the rating agencies onto the market. The removal of references within American and European legislation is a good thing, but the horse has long since left the stable. It is far too late to believe that the removal of references to ratings within legislation would have any effect at all. The systemic derailment took place and, unfortunately, rather than considering whether the rolling stock was efficient enough or suitable for the tracks laid for it, and also whether those laying the tracks were the right people for the job, what took place was the building of the very same track, with the very same rolling stock, right next to the smouldering wreckage of the last systemic derailment. It was business as usual very quickly afterwards and the rating agencies would continue on as before. Moody's had pressed home its oligopolistic advantage to the nth degree and not only lived to tell the tale, but it had also grown even more powerful as a result.

5.5 Conclusion

The GFC, years in the making, had laid several very uncomfortable truths out for everybody to see. The concept of 'too-big-to-fail' had unfortunately become part of the global lexicon, with the understanding the profits were to be privatised and losses left for the public to absorb, at the cost of crucial social services, an understanding that many would be forced to accept. In the credit rating arena, a critical transformation had occurred, and we are yet to see the true result of it; the credit rating agencies had seen of the worst the system had to throw at them and came out the other side, gleaming. Any arguments about the agencies being constrained by concerns of their 'reputational capital' were left in tatters as the years wore on after the GFC.

The rating agencies had consciously conspired against investors who they knew were being forced into the vehicles they alone, alongside their investment banker partners, were creating in their very own favour. They did this on an institutional, almost systematic scale. The $2 billion-odd that was clawed back in settlements represents a mere fraction of the fees the agencies earned for their role on the system that brought the western world to its knees. We saw how Moody's, given our public access to them, acted consciously in keeping analysts under pressure and without support, who manufactured methodologies, and who embarked on campaigns to infiltrate public opinion when there was nowhere left to turn. The post-Crisis congressional investigations paint the picture of an almost-criminal enterprise. It is perhaps concerning that the word 'criminal' does not appear anywhere in the many investigations where the credit rating agencies are concerned. Yet, in reality, there were very few laws broken, if any. This reality paints the picture of a systemic failure more than just a failure of the credit rating agencies.

The lack of an extensive, impactful, and reality-based regulatory framework for all of the years leading up to 2010 perhaps tells us that it is surprising that systemic failure at the hands of the credit rating agencies did not happen sooner, although as I have repeated on a number of occasions, the potential has always been there it just needed the environment to facilitate it. Yet, as you will see in the Afterword I have provided for you, there is nothing that the regulators can do, in reality. The systemic need for what the ratings provide is simply not dependent upon them being independent in reality, only in theory. The system does not care that the rating agencies colluded with issuers, because investors just simply continued on relying on the ratings after the Crisis. Sophisticated investors especially have never relied, and will never *rely*, on the ratings nor the information within them because, for the most part, their own research resources far outweigh that of the rating agencies (to suggest BlackRock and the like *need* the information rating agencies provides borders on the absurd); but, they absolutely do need the *signal* the ratings allow them to send and receive, and until there is an alternative to that signal production, the rating agencies will remain immensely profitable.

Notes

1   Tiberio Graziani, 'The Economic Crisis of the Western System' (2009) 13(3) World Affairs: The Journal of International Issues 14–21.
2   Dan Immergluck, 'High-Risk Lending and Public Policy, 1995–2008' in JR Tighe and Elizabeth J Mueller (eds), *The Affordable Housing Reader* (Routledge 2013) 1007.
3   Damon Silvers, 'Deregulation and the New Financial Architecture' in Martin H Wolfson and Gerald A Epstein (eds), *The Handbook of the Political Economy of Financial Crises* (OUP 2013) 439.
4   Jeffrey Friedman and Wladimir Kraus, *Engineering the Financial Crisis: Systemic Risk and the Failure of Regulation* (Pennsylvania UP 2011) 445.
5   Charles W Calomiris, 'Origins of the Subprime Crisis' in Asli Demirgüç-Kunt and others (eds), *The International Financial Crisis: Have the Rules of Finance Changed?* (World Scientific 2011) 88.
6   Charles W Calomiris, 'The Subprime Turmoil: What's Old, What's New, and What's Next' [2009 Spring] Journal of Structured Finance 6–52, 7.
7   Giovanni Dell'Ariccia and others, 'Policies for Macro-Financial Stability: Dealing with Credit Booms and Busts' in Stijn Claessens and others (eds), *Financial Crises: Causes, Consequences, and Policy Responses* (International Monetary Fund 2014) 328.
8   Peter J Wallison, 'Dissenting Statement' in Financial Crisis Inquiry Commission (ed), *Financial Crisis Inquiry Report* (GPO 2011) 451.
9   ibid 464.
10 Raghuram G Rajan, *Fault Lines: How Hidden Fractures Still Threaten the World Economy* (Princeton UP 2011).
11 James R Hagerty, *The Fateful History of Fannie Maw: New Deal Birth to Mortgage Crisis Fall* (The History Press 2012) 203.
12 Christopher Payne, *The Consumer, Credit and Neoliberalism: Governing the Modern Economy* (Routledge 2012) 169.
13 Financial Crisis Inquiry Commission, *Financial Crisis Inquiry Report* (GPO 2011) 113.
14 Immergluck (n 2) 216.
15 David Reiss, 'Subprime Standardisation: How Rating Agencies Allow Predatory Lending to Flourish in the Secondary Mortgage Market' (2006) 33 Florida State University Law Review 985, 988.

16 ibid 989.
17 Financial Crisis Inquiry Commission (n 13) 118.
18 Natalia Besedovsky, 'Financialisation as Calculative Practice: The Rise of Structured Finance and the Cultural and Calculative Transformation of Credit Rating Agencies' (2018) 16(1) Socio-Economic Review 61–84, 76.
19 Adam B Ashcraft, *Understanding the Securitisation of Subprime Mortgage Credit* (DIANE Publishing 2010) 12.
20 Besedovsky (n 18) 76.
21 Financial Crisis Inquiry Commission (n 13) 148.
22 U.S. Congress, *Wall Street and the Financial Crisis: The Role of Credit Rating Agencies* (GPO 2010) 297.
23 Besedovsky (n 18) 76.
24 U.S. Congress (n 22) 397.
25 Financial Crisis Inquiry Commission (n 13) 120.
26 ibid 121.
27 ibid 221.
28 U.S. Congress (n 22) 372.
29 Financial Crisis Inquiry Commission (n 13) 223.
30 U.S. Congress (n 22) 687.
31 Isabelle Huault and Chrystelle Richard, *Finance: The Discreet Regulator – How Financial Activities Shape and Transform the World* (Palgrave Macmillan 2012) 88.
32 Kenneth Dyson, *States, Debt, and Power: 'Saints' and 'Sinners' in European History and Integration* (OUP 2014) 360.
33 Eric Helleiner, 'The Financial Stability Board and International Standards' (2010) CIGI G20 Papers 1, 13.
34 Lucia Quaglia, *The European Union and Global Financial Regulation* (OUP 2014) 101.
35 ibid 102.
36 James Kwak, 'Financial Industry' in Joel Krieger and Craig N Murphy (eds), *The Oxford Companion to Comparative Politics* (OUP 2012) 415.
37 See Daniel I Castro, 'Structured Investment Vehicles (SIVs)' in Gary Strumeyer (ed), *The Capital Markets: Evolution of the Financial Ecosystem* (John Wiley & Sons 2017).
38 ibid 381.
39 Theodore R Malloch and Jordan D Mamorsky, *The End of Ethics and a Way Back: How to Fix a Fundamentally Broken Global Financial System* (John Wiley & Sons 2013) 134.
40 Complaint for Negligent Misrepresentation Under Common Law & California Civil Code §§ 1709 & 1710 & Negligent Interference with Prospective Economic Advantage at 23, Cal. Pub. Employees' *Ret Sys v Moody's Corp*, No. CGC-09-490241.
41 Daniel Cash, *Regulation and the Credit Rating Agencies: Restraining Ancillary Services* (Routledge 2018).

Conclusion

Thomas Friedman's almost famous quote about the strength of Moody's which opened the book, and which he has adapted on occasion owing to its popularity, is perhaps an appropriate way in which to also end this book now we know Moody's much better; that Moody's impact on the global scene is comparable to that of the US is, perhaps, accurate. Leaving aside the complexities that the quote does not address for one moment, this book has endeavoured to paint a picture of one credit rating agency in particular, in all its glory (or otherwise). The book, representing something in between a historical account and, at times, a seemingly fictional account(!), has taken us from the early stages of the American project, via its greatest heights, to its lowest lows. Throughout them all, the concept of rating, in its various guises, has synergistically played its part. Central to the modern development of that concept, Moody's provides with us a fascinating case study with which we can learn more about this unique, multi-faceted, complex, and critical industry.

We saw, time and time again, how the industry is no mere financial player; it is *the* gatekeeper for the modern world. A world within which securitisation and complex finance has led the world in a technological direction, the credit rating agencies have provided the theoretical protection needed to allow the machine to operate. However, ever since the concept was commercialised, we have seen an industry at odds with that social standing. We have seen an industry, almost, yearn to be freed of the pressure, expectation, and obligation that such a role brings with it, all whilst never shying away from the spoils that it brings also. We have seen extraordinarily powerful men carve the system into something akin to one of the key *natural* oligopolies that form integral parts of the modern human system, and crucially incorporate that into their operations. Key decisions made at critical junctures throughout the life of the company reveal to us some really interesting aspects we all must remember.

The company, perhaps as any company must, puts itself first. However, it is arguable that whilst societal trends have (ever so slowly) moved beyond that foundational understanding of a company's obligations towards a more progressive and sustainable viewpoint, Moody's and the other rating agencies have

DOI: 10.4324/9781003001065-6

remained resolute in their self-preservation. We can debate whether that stance is appropriate or not, and we can also debate whether it was necessary in the manner that Moody's and others did it. However, whilst I may suggest that the credit rating agencies protect themselves so vehemently is because they know full well their products are not that informationally sound nor useful, we saw just why it all does not matter. What the rating agencies offer does not find its value in its informational content; quite clearly, because with the rate of failure in the structured finance market alone, never mind anything else, the rating industry would not exist today. What the rating agencies offer is *systemically necessary* and once we understand that, everything else should fall into place.

The Afterword to this book describes the concept and applicability of signalling theory to the world of credit ratings. The ability to send and receive the right signal for the systemic positions key players hold is simply what the rating agencies bring to the party, and are compensated and protected accordingly. In the Dodd–Frank Act, the US Congress were abundantly clear that they wanted all references to the rating agencies out of federal statutes and financial regulations. The fact that this has not happened so long after the enactment of the Act tells us what the SEC cannot say to their congressional masters; credit ratings are fundamental within the current economic system. There is no alternative.

When we look back to John Moody and his development of the early companies which would eventually become the Moody's Investors Service we know today, his brilliance was his ability to iterate and build, to merge and develop, and to focus and apply. What came before him was a blueprint. It was almost a toolkit to dig into the lifeblood of the system that was developing around him. That system required the painfully simple, in order to make the painfully complex accessible. That an AAA rating is ostensibly better than a C rating is so incredibly simple and pure it is remarkable that it took until John to apply it, but apply it he did. We saw, throughout the book, that the system then morphed around what he had created. Whilst John's product was not always at the forefront of the system's usage of the concept, it was never far away. Now, as I write this, Moody's is still, consistently, referred to as a marker for development and almost a spearhead for the market which others can interpret. I am reminded of a recent story in the UK when a new Prime Minister promised radical tax changes; once Moody's made a public statement that it did not think the changes were wise and that markets would not react well, the Prime Minister was out of a job merely days later. Even the threat of a downgrade is enough in the sensationalised world that has developed.

John's development into a spiritual animal has always intrigued me. As we know, he came from a religious family and we saw how his early years were dominated by an internal struggle with his own understanding compared to his family's faith. I do not suggest that John turned to religion in the manner with which he did because of the impact he had made in the materialistic world, as he called it, but one wonders what he would make of the modern Moody's.

Controlled by one of the corporate titans he would have surely reviewed in one of his writings, the modern Moody's either represents the epitome of what John wanted, or the opposite. It has become a corporate monster that effectively controls societies, but the core mandate of supporting investors in their decisions, if that is what John truly believed in, has long since disappeared. The abandonment of such principles, if they ever existed, in the financial crisis saw to that. Perhaps it comes down to our reading of who John was and what he stood for, and I shall leave that to you without influence. One thing we do know for sure is that John's legacy will be continuing for some time yet, with more editions of this story likely needed in the future.

Afterword – The Signal Box

Given the importance of the railroad to Moody's and, therefore, to this book, I thought it appropriate to label this Afterword 'The Signal Box'. There is rationale in this chapter being separated from the order of the book's narrative, but it could have easily been interwoven into the fabric of the book. I separated it because the chapter could, if publication practices allowed, be attached to the end of every book I write on the credit rating agencies. It is appropriate and, as I hope you will agree upon reading it, helpful to include as a separate entity because it provides a direct answer to a question that almost everybody has when they encounter the credit rating space: if the credit rating agencies' products are not that informationally nutritious, and they have been identified by investigations the world over as being highly transgressive in their behaviour, why do they continue to be used? Why is it, on the back of their remarkable failure as the gatekeeper positioned to prevent what caused the Global Financial Crisis, that the rating agencies went on to become even richer, and their usage more widespread? Everything is antithetical, that is until you change the lens.

I have for a long time been a proponent of applying a particular theory to this problem of understanding the antithesis that defines the credit rating space (in truth, an antithesis that first inspired me to commit my career to understanding the credit rating space more). You will have seen me hint at the concept of signalling in different parts of the book, but I have introduced this application of Signalling Theory to the world of credit ratings on a number of occasions and do so again here. In the context of this book in particular, it will provide an extremely useful lens with which we can re-examine all that has come before this point in the book. I strongly believe, though I cannot ascertain it conclusively of course, that leading figures in our story absolutely recognised the conclusions that this Signalling lens provides, and acted accordingly. The brazen disregard for reputational damage suggests as much. It is more than just an understanding of one's oligopolistic position. It is the absolute understanding of one's *natural* oligopolistic position, one that cannot be changed. I have said it often, if anything major is to change in the credit rating system, it will mean that something *fundamental* has changed in the concept of capitalism, in the concept of modern life; credit rating agencies are simply integral to the modern world.

Many critics of the rating agencies will likely take umbrage at this suggestion, because it is uncomfortable to hear; something that causes so much damage can never be removed, unless one changes the entire system. It is uncomfortably true because the naturalness of the oligopolistic position the likes of Moody's enjoy is based upon a key service that is painfully simple in its utility. In providing what I think to be the neatest of descriptions of the wide field of signalling theory, Bird and Bird tell us that: signalling theory is concerned with how and why organisms exchange otherwise hidden information about each other or the world around them.[1] The scholars use the word organism here skilfully because, at its core, the theory is applicable to almost all walks of life wherever information asymmetry occurs; from peacock plumage to human resource departments, there is often an asymmetry to information that needs to be resolved before things move forward.[2] The term 'information asymmetry' simply describes an asymmetry, or imbalance, in what one thing knows against that of another.

Some of the world's most acclaimed minds have been credited with developing the theory of signalling, with many Nobel prizes being awarded to the forefathers and mothers of the discipline. Perhaps one of the most famous amongst them – George Akerlof – provides a simple example that demonstrates the root of the theory:

> Akerlof, in 1970, highlighted that the lemons problem could be represented by those situations in which buyers need to evaluate the quality of goods offered by sellers in a situation of information asymmetry. If buyers do not have enough information about the quality of goods sold, sellers of lower quality goods (lemons) can exploit the information asymmetry for themselves (moral hazard). In this situation, buyers could overestimate the price of lemons. As a consequence, the price of higher quality goods can become prohibitive. For sellers *not to be cheated* is to eliminate the information asymmetry, by signalling the higher quality of their products.[3]

In this scenario though, how does one send the signal to the consumer that the consumer can trust? If the seller of better produce simply informs that consumer that their produce is of a higher quality, the consumer has no reason to believe them. Furthermore, the consumer may even be distrustful of the signal, in that if one needs to tell you their produce is better without providing any evidence, then something likely is amiss. Another classic example which perhaps gets us closer to the world of credit ratings can be found from another of the founding members of the theory, Michael Spence:

> In his formulation of signalling theory, Spence utilized the labour market to model the signalling function of education. Potential employers lack information about the quality of job candidates. The candidates, therefore, obtain

education to signal their quality and reduce information asymmetries. This is presumably a reliable signal because lower quality candidates would not be able to withstand the rigors of higher education. Spence's model stands in contrast to human capital theory because he deemphasizes the role of education for increasing worker productivity and focuses instead on education as a means to communicate otherwise unobservable characteristics of the job candidate.[4]

This is potentially why we have different standards and categorisations of schools, particularly in the Higher Education sector; one University may be much more prestigious, have higher entry standards, and a more rigorous tutelage for the student, all resulting in, theoretically, a stronger signal that a degree holder from University A can send over a degree holder from University B. However, in this example, what if I, as the prospective employer, have literally no idea about the respective strengths and weaknesses of different universities? From this, we can see that one of the foundational issues to the concept of the signal is in the concept of there being different parties to that signal. With that in mind, it is of no surprise that 'management researchers have found that signalling effectiveness is determined in part by the characteristics of the receiver'.[5] In addition to this, Wolf argues that 'signalling theory operates with three elements: the signaller, the receiver, and the signal'.[6] This is true, but a more nuanced understanding requires us to interrogate that proclamation and we quickly see that more is needed.

If the theory consists of just three components, then what happens if the receiver cannot trust the signaller. The answer would be that the signal is rejected, but in reality, it is often critical that the relationship between the two is advanced, so there are only a few options that remain. If it is the signal that is not trusted, then the signaller will have the opportunity to send another signal. But, if the signal is not trusted, then will the signaller be again? Would the signaller risk sending the initial signal if they knew they only had one chance to get it right? Also, if we look at from the signaller's point of view, the signal may contain information that puts it at a distinct disadvantage; for example, what happens if the only way to communicate the signal is to do so in public, but the signal contains sensitive information? What if that sensitive information would put you at a competitional disadvantage? You can see here that even a cursory interrogation results in too many questions. The answer, as I have proposed elsewhere, is that the theory actually revolves around *four* key components: signaller, signal, trusted third-party, and receiver. Connelly et al. describe a number of phases in regard to the original three-stage composition of the theory, which are then evolved in the following:

- Signaller (person, product, or firm that has an underlying quality and needs to convince others of it);
- The signal is sent to the Receiver;

- The Receiver observes and interprets the signal. The Receiver then chooses the person, product, or firm if it is satisfied with the signal;
- Feedback is sent to the Signaller regarding their signal.

As I described above, in the scenario where the rejection of the signal is really not efficient for the running of a larger relationship (or system), then to move past the impasse the presence of a *trusted* third-party should be enough to resolve it:

- Signaller (person, product, or firm that has an underlying quality and needs to convince others of it);
- The information on the underlying quality is sent to a third-party;
- The third-party sends the signal to the Receiver;
- The Receiver observes and interprets the third-party's signal, and chooses to absorb the signal;
- Feedback is sent to the Signaller via investment (in whatever form).

That trusted third-party could be anything, ranging from a magazine that contains ratings, to food critics, to rating agencies. The theoretical importance is that the third-party is trusted enough to have the competency to deliver the signal in the necessary format, and to be independent enough to deliver the signal without representing the position of the original signaller. In this theoretical picture, for the third-party to be anything other than independent would skew the asymmetry back in the favour of the signaller and away from the receiver, thus returning the system back to one of inefficiency. In our example in this book, the credit rating agency as a fully private entity is wholly independent, and they inject the necessary resources into their methodological construction to be understood to be competent carriers of the signal between the signaller and receiver.

For the most part, this dynamic in the rating space is very simple: issuer of a debt needs to convince investors that they will pay back the debt, on time and in full. The credit rating agencies exist to determine the likelihood of that happening. That is the simple understanding. In reality, as we well know, things are more complicated. The biggest challenge to that independence, as I am sure you are asking yourself at this point, is what happens when the issuer of debt pays the credit rating agency to construct the rating. Surely, the issuer-pays remuneration model injects too much doubt for the investor, and the asymmetry returns to the relationship? This should, technically, be true but in reality, it is not, and to understand why we need to understand the environment around that dynamic more.

During the times of Lewis Tappan, an investor was a person. They invested their money and sought a return. They often used intermediaries to do it on their behalf, like a stockbroker for example, but in essence it was Person A investing Person A's resources. However, the development of the modern economy has seen the rise of a disassociation between one's position and the investment of their resources. The rise of disintermediation means that, for many, they will have others invest their money for them. The modern world is defined by the institutional investor, and with it, at its very core, the principal-agent relationship. The principal-agent relationship is based on trust and trust alone, but it is also based on fear. Perhaps they are one and the same thing, but nevertheless in the simplified scenario as me as a pension holder, that pension is what I need to retire with a certain level of stability and security (coincidentally, the lack of a social safety net is what led to Lewis Tappan collaborating with the avowed racist Benjamin Douglass, for fear of not having a nest-egg to retire with in his old age, but I digress); I obviously intend to guard that security as best I can. But, in the modern world, I need to have that retirement security built via investment throughout my working life, and to do that I need a professional investor. Those investors, especially for pensions, make up some of the world's largest companies holding trillions in 'assets under management' as they invest in markets so broad, they have become known as 'universal investors' – meaning, they invest so much they cannot take out of one market without shorting themselves in another. Think of the powerhouses of BlackRock, Vanguard, and State Street and you get the picture. With all this in mind, what actions could I take to protect my resources? One thing that would be perhaps easiest is to constrain the actions of my investment managers. At the same time, this massive investors risk causing systemic harm if they lose too much money, so what can the regulator do to prevent that? They also could restrict the investment managers to only invest in particular investments (just like the banking regulators did in the 1930s for the first time).

As a principal investor, I cannot tell my specialised investment managers what to invest in specifically. As a regulator, the *public* regulator could not tell the *private* investment manager what to invest in, specifically. Therefore, a particular format, or codification of the signal is required and it is that very understanding that lies at the heart of the credit rating agencies' social utility. The genius of John Moody was to transform the pioneering industrial model created by Lewis Tappan, inject the pioneering codification model developed by John Bradstreet, and marry it together to create *the rating scale*. Elegant in its simplicity, the rating scale can both hide the most complex and sensitive of information, but at the same time be understanding by everybody on the planet – AAA is higher than C. I could constrain my investment manager to only invest in securities rated BBB and above, for example, and regulators could constrain systemically-critical investment vehicles in only investing in AAA, which was the case before the Global Financial Crisis and remains so to this day.

Earlier I played the part of the reader and asked of the impact of the issuer-pays model on this utility of the credit rating agencies. Surely, being paid by the issuer reduces the trust the investor can have in the rating agencies to independently signal the creditworthiness of that same issuer? The answer, which I suspect John Moody knew, Arthur Whiteside of the National Credit Office knew, which Warren Buffett knows, and which almost everybody involves in the credit rating industry knows as well as the regulators tasked with regulating the industry knows, or should know, is that it simply does not matter. Whether the rating agency is 100% independent, 90%, or even 50%, it simply does not matter. As long as the rating agency does not go 100% into the category of being on the side of the signaller, everything will continue as normal because, quite simply, *it has to*. There is no alternative. When Buffett spoke of the need for his businesses to contain particular characteristics, chief amongst which was the ability to increase prices without the fear of significant loss of market share or unit volume, this was what he was referring to; can you push the limits of what is acceptable without suffering terminal damage? The answer for the credit rating agencies is a resounding 'yes' simply because there is nothing even close to an alternative; they have a captured market. This alone is the reason why in the aftermath of the Penn Central debacle, one that saw the National Credit Office fundamentally attack the position of its captured market (the investors), the victims went straight to the NCO's sister company when the NCO was removed from the scene. This alone is why even though the credit rating agencies were proven to have consciously acted against investors and sided with concentrated issuers by fraudulently distorting their stated models and processes, those same credit rating agencies are more utilised now and even richer than before. It is a foundational truth that, in the field of credit ratings, the agencies provide something for which there is absolutely no alternative and for which every market participant involved with debt or investment needs. Regulatory pushes to make investors do their own due diligence have not resulted in a decrease in credit rating utility. Regulatory pushes to remove regulatory reliance on credit ratings have not resulted in a decrease in credit rating utility. This is because those issues were never the reason why the ratings were used; they were used for wholly different purposes – they were used to signal.

The signal box is critical to every rail journey and as our own journey in this book comes to an end, the signal is critical for us too. It explains everything there is to know about credit rating agencies. Think back to everything you have read in this book and now apply this signalling lens to your understanding. For Moody's, and its evolution, I argue that what defines the successes it has experienced is that people connected to it have understood this lens before they take action, not only in reflection. By taking such actions in the knowledge that, come rain or shine the need for the credit ratings will remain, Moody's, its affiliates, and its competitors have been party to some of the most impactful and transformative events of the modern era in human history and, when we really understand the lens that I have just provided, they will likely be party to whatever fate has in store for us next.

Notes

1 Douglas W Bird and Rebecca Bliege Bird, 'Signalling Theory and Durable Symbolic Expression' in Bruno David and Ian J McNiven (eds), *The Oxford Handbook of the Archaeology and Anthropology of Rock Art* (OUP 2019) 347.

2 Patrick Bolton and Mathias Dewatripont, *Contract Theory* (MIT Press 2005) 126.

3 Sara Trucco, *Financial Accounting: Development Paths and Alignment to Management Accounting in the Italian Context* (Springer 2015) 26.

4 Brian L Connelly and others, 'Signaling Theory: A Review and Assessment' (2011) 37(1) Journal of Management 39–67, 42. For Spence's work see: Michael Spence, 'Job Market Signalling' (1973) 87 Quarterly Journal of Economics 355–74.

5 ibid.

6 Sandra Wolf, *Signaling Family Firm Identity: Family Firm Identification and Its Effects on Job Seekers' Perceptions About a Potential Employer* (Springer 2017) 32.

Index

Printed in the United States
by Baker & Taylor Publisher Services